13 STEPS TO OPTIMUM SELF ESTEEM FOR WOMEN

A COMPLETE GUIDE TO INCREASING SELF-WORTH AND NEVER HAVING TO DOUBT YOURSELF AGAIN

SARRANA RAIN

A Special Gift To Our Readers

Included with your purchase of this book is a copy of our listicle, How To Be You.

If you somehow feel discontented of what you have or discouraged because you believe you are unworthy, not enough, not capable, think again.

If you think you need to keep up, be 'some' one to be accepted, to be valuable, to be loved, think again.

Discover THE SECRET to achieving pure happiness and unfaltering confidence given the pressure of our new generation's evolving social scripts and standards through this mini-book, How To Be You.

It is a good read for you and for all the women you care about.

Stop living someone else's life.

Live not FOR someone but for YOU, for your happiness and your cause.

Scan the QR code or visit the link below and let us know which email address to deliver it to.

http://sarrana-rain.com/

https://arvieiguanaltd.activehosted.com/f/3

CONTENTS

PART II
The Skills You Need To Level Up or Dial Down Your
Self-Esteem

VISION

Women, they just have to see things in a new light, then there is the better world waiting for them, a world full of compassion wherein they can strive to hone their abilities and uniqueness, live mindfully with inner peace, make things happen with courage and will, be themselves the master of their own self—gentle but dauntless, resilient and driven, exist with a sense of purpose, cultivate love to self and others, respects self while respecting others.

INTRODUCTION

I once dated a scientist, someone who was smart, charismatic. I adored him so much that his ways of living soon became my own. We were only seeing each other for a few years, yet it already felt like he had become my pillars. He was a best friend and a family to me. One day he had to leave, and so my world fell apart.

His words before saying goodbye, "You have to fill your own cup, so do I."

He was right, so I just let him go.

I fell in love many times, and each break up hit me every time.

I thought I had become empty, but no, I was wrong.

The truth is, I no longer had the capacity to contain.

I was broken into pieces that I couldn't hold anything anymore, not even a single drop of love for my own self.

Should I blame it on love?

Should we blame it on love? Should we blame it on other people that we are miserable, that we are hurt, that we are incomplete, that we are lonely?

Or could it be that we are missing one very important thing?

I am talking about fixing our self-esteem, or self-worth or self-regard or self respect, as they call it.

As women, we often forget our real value. We fall short on confidence and the belief that we can actually obtain almost anything and can be solely responsible for our own genuine happiness and prosperity, without anyone owing this to us.

You may be intoxicating yourself with the thoughts that you are not enough, and not good enough, then you doubt your abilities, your looks, your body, your career, your relationships.

It is the lack of self-esteem that causes you to not speak up for yourself, that you shy away. It is this lack that makes you afraid to take up space. It is the lack of self belief that you fear. It is the lack of self-worth that you forget the meaning of your existence. Lack of it is destructive, however, with too much of it, you meet the same end.

As a person for whom cultivating self-esteem has been a life challenge—I feel you, very deeply, and I understand you the most. Our universe has intertwined today. If you're wondering about how our stories relate to each other, you can find it at the end of this book but, for now, let's focus on you first.

What you are about to learn from my book helped me restore my self-worth that consequently created space for me to make it to the next level which is: serving my purpose and creating abundance.

I am passionate about helping anyone in need to uplift herself from sinking to become her best version. And I have figured that my purpose is to give you a helping hand.

Cultivating healthy self-esteem is not a subject taught in school nor a course you can take in college. It is a lifetime learning process. A lot of people fail to recognize that this is a discipline they can actually study and master to attain the state of being mentally strong, succeeding all adversities life may bring.

After years of soulful quest and obsessive research, I have finally put together all the wisdom I have learned and from it, formulated the steps for you to take that will help you reach the optimum level of self-esteem—the unconditional, strong, and stable kind of self-worth.

Here Is Your At-a-Glance 13-Step Program to Develop a Strong and More Robust Self-Esteem That Will Last You a Lifetime.

PART I

The first part of the book will help you understand the importance of self-esteem, how it forms, and what has happened to yours.

Step 1: Understand Self-Esteem And How It Matters To You

Step 2: Change The Way You Feel About Yourself

PART II

In this second part of the book, the real work starts—levelling up (or down) your self-esteem so you can live a happier, healthier and more stable life.

Step 3: Level Up Your Confidence

Step 4: Raise Your Inner Voice

Step 5: Face Your Fears

Step 6: Be Kind To Yourself

Step 7: Love Your Body

Step 8: Connect to Your Inner Peace

Step 9: Master Your Emotion

Step 10: Dump Your Old Insecurities

PART III

This final part of the book is all about enjoying the benefits of a stable and healthy level of self-esteem that will support you through whatever life throws your way!

Step 11: Heal. Let Go. Move Forward

Step 12: Take Control

Step 13: Know Your Real Value

Work your way through each of the 13 steps in this book and I promise you'll find just the right level of self-esteem to move through whatever life throws your way without giving up your feelings of self-worth.

You'll have all the answers to the questions that will now be starting to bubble up (and more) by the time you've worked through all 13 steps in this book but to start, let's start with Step 1 and find out what we really mean when we talk about self-esteem and understand why it really matters.

PART I

UNDERSTANDING SELF-ESTEEM

STEP 1 (PART 1)

UNDERSTAND SELF-ESTEEM AND HOW IT MATTERS TO YOU

"The most beautiful people we have known are those who have known defeat, known suffering, known struggle, known loss, and have found their way out of the depths. These persons have an appreciation, a sensitivity and an understanding of life that fills them with compassions, gentleness, and a deep loving concern. Beautiful people do not just happen."

— ELIZABETH KUBLER-ROSS, PSYCHIATRIST
AND PIONEER OF OUR UNDERSTANDING OF
THE STAGES OF GRIEF

Self-esteem, or self-worth or self-respect, is something we all need to help us overcome the challenges life throws our way. It is like a secret tool in our box of life skills—one that will help us to find a way of being comfortable in our own skin, around other people and in the world.

But it's maybe not something not many people ever stop and think about much.

This is a shame because once you know more about self-esteem— what it is and why it is so important in helping us to have a happy and meaningful life—then you will also realize it is something you can work on and you should work on.

You can, literally, learn how to boost your feelings or self-worth or, if you are in danger of overdoing the confidence thing, take them down a notch or two.

Only you will know the exact level of self-esteem that feels right and works for you.

Of course, you may find that this level changes as you get older and have more life experience under your belt. That's why I talk about an "optimum" level in this book: not too much, not too little, but just the right amount of self-esteem so that you will feel more comfortable with yourself and when you are around and interacting with other people.

Can you guess why I have opened Step One with a quote about struggle and suffering? It's because, as you work your way through each of the 13 steps designed to help you, you will discover that the level you are starting with will be a direct result of two things:

1. What has happened to you in your life so far.
2. How you managed and coped with what has happened to you in your life so far.

The first thing to get clear is that things that you may have absolutely no control over could end up deciding your self-worth. What kind of things do I mean? Well, you may have had just the right level of self-esteem as a child but ended up with a lot less after one of your parents walked out. Or maybe you were bullied at school or had to deal with some form of body shaming which left you socially isolated. Maybe you faced serious racism or have struggled with mental health difficulties.

If you are older and thinking back to things that have happened in your life, you may be able to better see how whatever self-esteem you started out with may have crashed overnight after life tripped you up one way or another.

Some of the reasons your self-esteem can take a hit are:

- Difficult work situations and/or relationships
- Bullying
- Feeling stigma which could be about your gender identification or just where you live
- Social isolation due to shyness or being new to a place
- Being physically challenged in some way that means you feel like an "outsider"
- Mental health issues
- Racism and other types of prejudice from others
- Rejection in close relationships, family, or romantic ones
- Being a single parent
- Living alone following the breakdown of a relationship or the death of partner
- Loneliness
- Being single when you want to find your soulmate and start a family

- Feeling you have failed at everything
- And many more, including things we couldn't even put into words

Go back over the list above and tick those events that have already happened in your life. You can now see for yourself how fragile self-esteem can be when we take it for granted and don't take the time to nurture and support it and how vulnerable our feelings about our self-worth are to "knocks" from the outside world—including, and especially, other people's actions and decisions.

By the end of Step One, you will understand one very important thing because you'll know that everything that has shaped your life so far, including who you were born to, how you were raised, and who you've already loved or lost has had an impact on how you now feel about YOU!

DOES ANYONE EVER ASK YOU "HOW'S YOUR SELF-ESTEEM?"

I bet the answer is "No, nobody ever asked me about that!"

They (and I'm talking about people like parents, teachers, family, and friends) may have mentioned things like ambition and goals and self-respect and motivation and drive, but did anyone (until now) ever sit you down and check in on your self-esteem and how you really feel about yourself and your life story so far?

In fact, never mind other people. When did you last check in on your own feelings of self-worth and self-esteem?

Have you *ever* stopped to ask: "How am I really feeling about myself?"

Isn't it odd how nobody really talks about something that is so important it will shape just about every decision to make in your life: from who you partner with to what work you'll choose to do.

All those big life-changing decisions decided by two little words made into one: self-esteem!

So, let's get started and dive right in to learn everything we can about self-esteem and what it really means.

WHAT IS SELF-ESTEEM?

What are we really talking about when we use the phrase self-esteem? Who has it, who doesn't? Can we measure it and once we know what we're talking about, how can we take better care of it?

First, we'll do a quick history check to learn who first started thinking and talking about self-esteem, and then we'll come bang up to date so we know what mental health doctors, psychologists, and other academics mean when they use the term today.

In intellectual circles, the phrase self-esteem was first used by a highly respected Scottish philosopher and enlightenment thinker David Hume, who lived in the 1770s.

He was the first academic "thinker" who identified the importance of valuing and thinking well of yourself. And he said the reason this is so important is that those who had good self-esteem would be much more likely to reach their full potential in life.

Even better than that, they would, he said, be more likely to want to do good things and not just for themselves, but for others too.

Hume's ideas divided people because he also argued that there is no permanent "self" which remains unchanged throughout our lives.

He was certain that people can—and do—change over their lifetime.

This is really important for you to hear because it means those with lower self-esteem can learn ways of changing that and of achieving higher levels of self-esteem. And equally, those with too much self-esteem (yes, you can have too much of a good thing, and we'll explore that idea later) can also learn how to moderate and move toward an optimum level of self-worth.

Notice how another way of describing self-esteem just crept into our text there: self-worth.

Some people use the terms self-esteem, self-worth, self-respect interchangeably, and these are all good words to focus on. If you have a pen and paper somewhere nearby, jot them down. I know we all work on computers but handwriting important or key words is a really good way to get an idea ingrained in your mind.

So, here are your key words—and what they mean—from Step One:

Esteem—*defined as having respect and admiration.*

Worth—*defined as the level at which someone, or something, deserves to be valued or rated.*

Respect—*a feeling of deep admiration for someone or something elicited by their abilities, qualities or achievements.*

WHAT HAPPENED NEXT?

It would be another 100 years or so before self-esteem earned its place as a distinct field of psychological study.

By this time, a psychologist and anthropologist working in the late 1800s—a man called William James—had identified two distinct aspects of the self.

He called these the "I" self and the "Me" self.

The "I" self, he said, is a subject of its experiences and is made up of three further distinctions which are the social self, the material self and the spiritual self.

The "Me" self, though, is an object of experience. So, you could think of this as being the "me" you feel deep down, who you really are and the one you don't show to too many people.

The word "*self*" comes from Old English meaning "one's own person."

And of the social, material and spiritual selves that James talked about, it is the social self that most closely relates to the concept of self-esteem we have today.

This in itself, tells us something else that is important too.

Our level of self-esteem can be an "outcome" of our social inter-actions.

It does not exist in and of itself alone.

Which takes us back to the idea that what happens to you—and now we can add, how people treat you—will determine your starting levels of self-esteem.

By the middle of the swinging sixties, self-esteem as an academic field really hit its stride.

This was the decade that the social psychologist, Morris Rosenberg, gave us a proper definition of self-esteem as "a feeling of self-worth."

He also came up with a way to measure people's levels of self-worth using what became known as the Rosenberg self-esteem scale (RSES).

And finally, after about 300 years since those early philosophers first started talking about the importance of self-worth, it looked as if the study of self-esteem was here to stay.

But that all changed at the turn of the 20th century when the behavioral scientists re-categorized psychology as an experimental science (no different from the study of biology and chemistry).

At that point, nobody thought to conduct clinical trials on self-esteem, and so for about 50 years, all went very quiet on the self-worth front.

Then, in the middle of the 20th century, the pendulum swung back in favor of exploring and understanding the value of self-esteem, especially in both the diagnosis and treatment of mental health issues.

Psychologists now understood once again that self-esteem plays a key role in how people feel about themselves, how they measure their own worth, how they navigate life's challenges, or how they become so discouraged (low self-esteem) they need help to find to reach that potential (their potential) that the enlightened philosopher Hume first talked about.

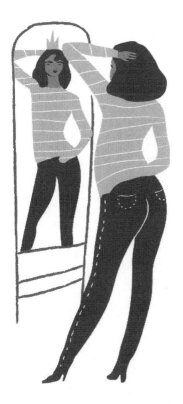

WHO HAS IT?

You do. Even on the days it feels like you have none. You have it, you've just misplaced it. We saw in our quick review of the history of the study of self-esteem that the value of feelings of self-worth are recognized by clinicians as being positive and helpful in dealing with life's challenges.

In the late 1960s, the Canadian/American psychotherapist Nathaniel Branden maintained that your self-esteem is made up of two distinct components:

1. **To consider yourself effective:** trust in your ability to

think, learn and to choose and make correct decisions and
to overcome challenges and produce changes.

2. **To respect oneself:** the confidence in your right to be
   happy, and the confidence that you are worthy of the
   respect, love, and self-fulfillment appearing in your life.

By the 2000s, these ideas had been distilled down into two simpli-
fied components: competence and worth. Robert Reasoner, the
author of *"Building Self-Esteem"* went on to explain that based on
these two components, *"Self-esteem is the experience of being capable of
meeting life's challenges and being worthy of happiness!"*

The one thing all the researchers agree on is that the formation of
self-esteem is a long process and one that will involve periods when
you "fall over" and feel as if you have failed.

Falling Down
Is Part of Life
Getting Back Up
Is Living

— JOSE N. HARRIS

Remember the list earlier of all the ways in which your self-esteem
can take a proper battering? Imagine if, instead of feeling you've
failed each time something bad happens, you were to see it as an
opportunity to pick yourself back up, live your life, and show the
world what you are really made of. The key word here is "opportunity" because what we are understanding now is that without these
life challenges, your self-esteem cannot get established and grow
through your life.

STATES OF SELF-ESTEEM

It was important to me to get the title of this book just right because when you talk about self-esteem, people automatically think only of those suffering from low self-esteem or self-worth. And yes, there will be a lot of advice as we work through the 13 steps to find our "optimum" level of self-esteem for those whose self-worth feel crushed or even missing and who may be prone to feeling anxious and even depressed. But it is important to realize that there is such a thing as having too much self-esteem too and when that's the case, there is another condition that will raise its ugly head: narcissism.

There is, if you like to think of it this way, a scale of self-esteem with narcissism at the top and low self-esteem at the bottom of that scale. What we will be doing in this book is finding our way to an "optimum" level of self-esteem and to work out what is the right level for you. Let's take a look at the three very different types of self-esteem so you identify which one relates to you and how you really feel about yourself.

You can easily work out which state applies to you by answering the simple question for each state.

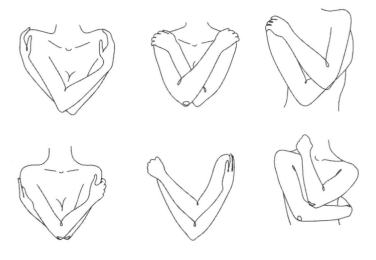

Shattered Self-Esteem

Q. Do you feel lovable?

If your answer to this question is "no", then you are suffering from a shattered self-esteem. You will feel you have no inherent value and may feel overwhelmed by defeat and/or shame. Our self-esteem often takes a big hit during times of "normal" life stage transitions, so it may be you have just hit your 30s (or your 50s) and feel sad you've not achieved more by now. If you are a bit older you may start using phrases like "*Well, I'm old now*" and only speak out to insult and bring yourself and your achievements to date down. You may feel crippled by sadness and self-pity. This is a hard place to be and can feel hopeless.

Vulnerable

Q. Do you refuse to take part in games to avoid feeling crushed if you lose?

Superficially, your self-esteem is in good shape but if the answer to this question is "yes" then, with you, what you see is not what you get! You have a positive self-image and most people wouldn't guess at the fact that, while it looks good, your self-esteem is fragile and likely to crumble at the first proper challenge it faces. Deep down, you know the truth about this and for those getting to know you, there are tell-tale signs of a self-esteem that is vulnerable. You may be someone who stays away from others, pretending you don't need family or friends, or you may deliberately lose a game so you can make out that winning doesn't matter to you anyway. If you are someone who blames everyone else for their failures, you may be dealing, behind scenes, with a vulnerable self-esteem.

Strong

Q. If you were to lose everything overnight and wake up tomorrow with no job and no relationship, would you think less of yourself or blame others?

If your answer to this question is "no", then your self-esteem is strong. People with strong self-esteem can navigate their way through life's knocks and disappointments without losing their sense of self-worth. These people often come across as humble and cheerful. They'll fight hard to achieve their goals, but they won't think their lives are over when they fail. A loss of social prestige won't cripple them because they know they can be happy without having to impress others, and they understand what's more important are the feelings of well-being that comes from having strong levels of self-esteem. These are the people who can own up to their own mistakes because doing so does not knock their self-esteem or make them feel they no longer matter.

You will know now which of these three types of self-esteem best describe how you feel about yourself right now and which apply to other people in your life. But it is important to also know that even the strongest of strong, self-esteem is not indestructible—and so in the same way you can learn to recalibrate your current levels of self-esteem you can also fall from a strong level down to a vulnerable or even low level, depending on what happens to you and how others react to you.

IN THE NEXT CHAPTER

We'll take a look at the origins of self-esteem so we can better understand how it takes shape in our own lives and to see why we may end up having too much or too little

2

STEP 1 (PART 2)

THE FORMATION OF SELF-ESTEEM

We're going to take a short break from my 13-step program in this chapter to take a closer look at the life-long processes involved in the formation of self-esteem and the different types of self-esteem that have been identified by psychologists and other researchers.

Once we understand that self-esteem is not a fixed characteristic—in the way, say, the color of your eyes is fixed—but something where levels fluctuate throughout our lives, then we can see the importance of acquiring those skills which I will outline in the upcoming chapters. Understanding this means we can "level up" (or dial down) our self-esteem to just the right level.

In this chapter, we will learn that self-esteem can take a serious dip at different developmental stages in our lives, especially in the teenage and young adulthood stages.

THE DEVELOPMENT OF SELF-ESTEEM

All the academic research to date points to one thing—the most critical life stage when it comes to the development of your self-esteem is during adolescence. We understand now that self-esteem forms over a long period and is closely linked with both your self-image and your self-conscience, and researchers now understand that the formation of self-esteem is inextricably entwined with periods in our lives when it feels like things are going wrong and nothing is going our way.

The academics refer to this as "periods of downfall," which happen to us all, but which they have discovered are likely to be more common when we transition from one life stage to another, say from the end of our teens to young adulthood or from midlife to eventual retirement and old age. What this tells us is that self-esteem is also closely linked to status and where we see ourselves in the social pecking order.

WHERE DO YOU STAND—RIGHT NOW—IN THAT PECKING ORDER?

If you had to say where you think you stand in that social pecking order right now what would you say? Would you be able to put your hand on your heart and report that you feel seen and heard and valued and respected by not only those you care about and love but those you work and socialize with too? Or do you feel the polar opposite to all those things; unseen, unheard, disrespected, and unvalued by all those who matter to you?

If your teenage years are a recent or even a distant memory, think back to those perhaps turbulent times and ask yourself the same question. Did you feel seen, heard, valued, and respected? I suspect the answer, for many of you, will be "*no*', or "*not much.*" I am asking you to take yourself back to that time of your life to remember how you felt about yourself and your perceived status so you can really see just how strongly big life changes and transitions can shape our levels of self-esteem.

Research shows that having taken a serious dip in the teenage phase, self-esteem usually levels back up in young adulthood and again, we can see why this might be just by thinking about what was likely happening to you at that time in your life or, if you are in your twenties and thirties, right now.

You may have landed the job of your dreams or be living with a partner you love, you may be thinking of starting a family or hoping to take time to travel extensively before you become more tied by responsibilities. You may have just left home and are now enjoying the freedoms of independence or you may be training for work that feels (and is) meaningful to you. There are so many "positives" we can associate with this phase of our lives, you could probably write a long list here of your own which will be unique to you.

Now, compare this with what was happening when you hit your teens.

Perhaps you felt you had woken up one morning in some strange limbo land where you were no longer a child and not yet an independent adult which meant nobody really knew the right way to treat you. Perhaps the world looked a little bit scary, and there were times you wanted to hang on to the safety of childhood or perhaps your childhood had not been safe and you couldn't wait to transit into young adulthood and all the freedoms that would bring with it.

If I asked you to list all the things that were positive about being a teenager would your list be as long as the list of positives you could write for young adulthood, even with all its challenges? I suspect not. And so, if I then asked you when did you feel best about yourself, as a teenager or as a young adult, you will probably give an answer that reflects what the science tells us and say you have, or had, more self-esteem as a young adult than as a teen. That is not to say you automatically have, or had, the right level, just that you most likely have more than when your self-esteem was seriously challenged just by being a teenager.

ENCOURAGING SELF-ESTEEM IN ADOLESCENCE

A working model that helps us understand the formation and ongoing development of self-esteem is one which makes two key assumptions, namely:

1. Self-esteem forms early in life and in response to both key relationships and a person's temperament
2. Once formed, high self-esteem gives you the ability to promote, protect, and restore your feelings of self-worth.

Numerous studies emphasize the essential role of the family environment in the formation of your personality, especially in early childhood and in adolescence, it has been shown that parental interest and involvement, and having parents who are willing to give their teenagers autonomy and freedom, correlates strongly to high levels of self-esteem in teens.

Researchers pinpoint adolescence as being a critical period in the formation of self-esteem, and there is no question that low self-esteem through the teenage years will be mirrored in behavior at home and at school. Similarly, high levels of self-esteem play out through a teen's choices and behaviors.

SIGNS OF HIGH/HEALTHY SELF-ESTEEM IN ADOLESCENCE

- The teenager with high self-esteem can positively influence both the opinion and behavior of others
- They can tackle new situations positively and confidently
- They have a high level of tolerance toward feelings of frustration
- They accept early responsibilities
- They can correctly assess a situation
- They communicate positive feeling about themselves
- They demonstrate good self-control
- They believe the things they experience are a result of their own choices and behaviors

If these are all the ways in which positive self-esteem shows up during adolescence, then it makes sense the polar opposite beliefs and behaviors will be a sign of poor/low self-esteem and you can then very quickly see how low self-esteem can threaten and endanger an adolescent's ability to regulate their emotions. And if high self-esteem works to promote resilience and health adaptation to new circumstances, low self-esteem does the opposite.

SIGNS OF LOW/POOR SELF-ESTEEM IN ADOLESCENCE

- The teenager with low self-esteem does not believe they can positively influence either the opinion or the behavior of others
- They cannot tackle new situations either positively or confidently
- They have low tolerance toward feeling of frustration
- They don't accept early responsibilities
- They make incorrect assessment of situations
- They don't communicate positive feelings about themselves
- They demonstrate poor self-control and poor regulation of their own emotions
- They believe the bad things they experience are the fault of others and fail to make the connection with their own choices and behaviors

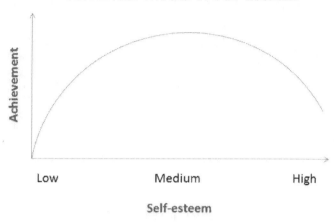

THE CURVILINEAR MODEL OF SELF-ESTEEM

The curvilinear model of self-esteem is one researchers use to pinpoint where the levels lie and to demonstrate the optimum level of self-esteem lies in the middle of the curve (as shown above).

Let's look at a few more of the behavior comparisons which reveal why levelling up (or down) to just the right amount of self-esteem is important for a happy and healthy life.

People with high self-esteem focus on growth and achievement whereas people with low self-esteem focus on trying to not make mistakes in life which can be limiting. Low self-esteem has been linked with multiple negative outcomes including a higher risk of depression, feeling more troubled by failure, and being more likely to interpret events as "negative" even when they are not. For example, someone with poor self-esteem will often hear a non-critical comment made by someone else as being critical of them and those with low self-esteem have also been shown to feel shy in social settings, self-conscious, and unable to express themselves. As well as causing higher levels of social anxiety, low self-esteem has even been linked by empirical evidence to an increased risk of pregnancy.

When school counsellors were asked by researchers to list five characteristics that best describe students with low self-esteem of the 1000+ words supplied, the most common words that were used are these:

1. Withdrawn/shy/quiet
2. Insecure
3. Underachieving
4. Negative (attitude)
5. Unhappy
6. Socially inept
7. Angry/hostile
8. Unmotivated
9. Depressed
10. Dependent/follower
11. Poor self-image
12. Non-risk-taker
13. Lacks self-confidence
14. Poor communication
15. Acts out

LOW SELF-ESTEEM IN CHILDREN

It is reported that, on average, self-esteem in children is relatively high but there are, of course, exceptions and children who suffer from poor self-esteem from a very young age. In these children, key factors for such a poor self-image include the threat of physical punishment and the withholding of love and affection by the parents/parental figures. When this happens, a child will learn they only get positive validation (and a boost to their self-esteem) if they act in a certain and approved way.

Unfortunately, children who suffer from low self-esteem will often act out in ways that should alert their carers to the issues, including bullying, quitting, cheating, and avoiding challenges that they worry they may fail at. These counterproductive behaviors become coping strategies but equally, a child with low self-esteem may be more vulnerable to bullying, less resistant to peer pressure and may seem withdrawn or shy. Another behavior that signals low levels of self-esteem in a child is that they struggle to have fun with their friends.

THE ADOLESCENT GENDER GAP

We've already seen in this chapter that self-esteem takes a nose dive during adolescence which researchers put down to a decline in positive body image and other factors linked to puberty, but there is also a gender gap that begins to emerge with adolescent boys reporting higher levels of self-esteem than adolescent girls. We will take a look, at the end of this chapter, more closely at the formation of self-esteem for females, but if you have ever been an adolescent girl, then you will already understand the pressures, and researchers warn that those girls who feel pressured to achieve the idealised perfect body image as shown in Western media are those who are most vulnerable to suffering from low levels of self-esteem. Nobody can live up to these ideals, unless they succumb to airbrushing, but that doesn't stop teenage girls from feeling like failures because they are striving but failing to achieve the impossible!

TYPES OF SELF-ESTEEM

We saw in chapter one how someone's self-esteem will fall into one of three categories: (1) strong and stable (2) vulnerable or (3) shattered but there are further definitions which it is worth taking a little time to understand. It will then be this foundation of understanding that we work from in Part II, where we explore how to level up (or dial down) our levels of self-esteem to find just the right optimum level.

Contingent vs Non-Contingent Self-Esteem

Contingent definition: "occurring or existing only if certain circumstances are the case."

The definition of the word contingent tells us something important for understanding the difference in these two types of self-esteem, it tells us that one type of self-esteem depends on something else (is contingent on) and the other does not (is unconditional). So, now we need to ask well, what does contingent self-esteem depend on?

It depends (is contingent on) external sources and circumstances. In other words, you have far less control over how you feel about yourself if you are basing your self-worth, self-value, and self-esteem on factors outside your control such as what other people say and think about you.

Relationships, family, friends and work ones come into play here because these are the people whose comments can make or break your day and sense of self-worth. When your self-esteem is contingent on approval and applause from other people then when you don't get it, your feelings of self-worth and self-value will slump.

The hallmarks of contingent self-esteem include instability, unreliability, and vulnerability, and you can see why: if you base your self-esteem on the opinions of others, you are giving yourself no say in the matter. This also means you are condemning yourself to a lifetime of pursuing self-esteem as a measure of what others think about you. Any self-esteem that is based on approval is doomed to fail;

nobody is perfect and nobody receives constant approval from those that matter to them. This then sets up a cycle of certain failure and can trigger serious mental health challenges, including depression. It can also mean you find yourself avoiding those activities and life choices that you fear others may not approve of. It takes courage to be yourself, whatever your circumstances and stage of life, but when your self-esteem is contingent on the approval of others it can make the journey to self-acceptance (and, as a result, higher self-esteem) longer and more painful than it needed to be.

If contingent self-esteem depends on the opinions of others then non-contingent self-esteem has its roots elsewhere.

Non-contingent self-esteem is described as true, stable, and solid.

There is a really simple way to understand how and why non-contingent differs from contingent self-esteem and that is that with non-contingent self-esteem, you have a core belief that you are acceptable.

We could spend a long time with that one word: acceptable.

It means that you truly believe you are good enough, just as you are.

Let's repeat that. JUST AS YOU ARE.

It does not mean you are ok "*if*" ... or "*because*" ... or you will be "*when*" ...

There are no conditions attached to this type of self-esteem which you can think of as being complete self-acceptance. You are accept-able for being you, the way you are and the way you always have been. No changes required so you can feel valued and trusted and that there is a place in the world for you.

You are accepted. UNCONDITIONALLY.

If you are reading this book, then this type of self-esteem and the words used to describe may seem like I have suddenly flipped into using another language. It may not have ever occurred to you that you are both acceptable and accepted, just the way you are and this may be what lies at the very root of your low self-esteem which we will explore now.

HAVING LOW SELF-ESTEEM

There are just so many different factors that can impact your self-esteem and leave you with a contingent version of self-worth—the one that says you have to do this or be that in order to be accepted and acceptable, and to claim your rightful place in the world. We ran through some of these factors in chapter one but there are more, including your family story, your physical appearance, your weight, your socioeconomic status, your emotional experiences which can feel like failures—as I said, the list goes on and on. And if this applies to you then you will recognize, in yourself, some of the behaviors (below) which often signals low self-esteem in those that act out this way.

Behaviors that Indicate Low Self-Esteem:

- Highly self-critical
- Dissatisfied with yourself and your life
- Hypersensitive to criticism, leading to feelings of resentment of those being critical and feelings of being attacked unfairly
- Chronic indecision
- Exaggerated fear of making mistakes
- People-pleasing tendencies and an unwillingness to displease others
- Setting unobtainable perfectionism as an unrealistic goal

- Feeling frustrated when perfectionism is not achieved
- Feeling guilty about and dwelling on past mistakes
- Exaggerating the magnitude of past mistakes
- Feeling hostile and defensive and irritable, often with no provocation and for no reason
- Feeling pessimistic about life and your own future
- Showing a negative outlook
- Feeling envious or resentful of those you see as being "better" than you or "better off"
- Catastrophizing by seeing temporary setbacks as intolerable conditions

That's quite some list to beat yourself with when the real reason you are struggling is poor or low self-esteem. It's ironic how, at a time when you need to be kinder to yourself, you will be more critical and when it has never been more important to develop non-contingent self-esteem, you will be busy chasing the approval and praise of others, without which you cannot muster any self-worth. You may even believe that people will only like you if you are a success and so end up hiding your perceived failures, instead of seeking help.

I think there's no argument that suffering from low self-esteem is a recipe for misery and will only work to undermine your resilience and ability to cope with the challenges life throws your way over the long term. So, let's get reinspired by examining all the benefits of having a stable, healthy and non-contingent type of self-esteem.

HIGH/HEALTHY SELF-ESTEEM

These people know who they are. They don't change, depending on which group of friends they find themselves spending time with and they don't ditch their core values in order to please others and court some kind of meaningless popularity and win that pointless contest. Here are some of the clues you can spot in others which tell you their self-esteem is pretty high and intact and is "the thing" that lies at the core of their resilience.

People with Healthy Levels of Self-Esteem:

- Have firm core values and principles which they live by and will defend in the face of opposition. That said, they are also secure enough in their self-worth to modify their beliefs in the light of new experiences
- Trust their own judgements, even when others don't approve of their choices
- Do not feel guilty when others think they are making a wrong choice
- Do not spend excessive amounts of time either worrying about what is past or what lies in the future. They show an intense ability to live in the present
- Trust in their own ability to solve problems
- Do not become derailed by failures or other difficulties but treat them as learning experiences
- Ask for help when they need it
- Consider themselves an equal in dignity, even if their circumstances differ wildly from others they do not adopt an inferior or superior position but accept we all have different talents, prestige, and financial standing
- Understand they are an interesting person and of value to those with whom they have a relationship or friendship

- Can resist manipulation
- Only collaborate with others if it is convenient and appropriate
- Can admit to difficult feelings when they have them
- Can enjoy positive feelings when they have them
- Are able to enjoy a diverse range of activities and can find fun in life
- Show sensitivity to the needs and feelings of others
- Generally, accept society's rule for the good of the collective
- Do not seek to prosper at the expense of someone else
- Can voice discontent without belittling themselves or others when challenges do arise
- Understand the difference between confidence and arrogance
- Is not a people-pleaser
- Does not base their self-worth on the approval of others
- Knows how to set boundaries

Looking at this impressive list of attributes—which also highlights just how positively a healthy self-esteem will shape and influence life —we can also see there is a really important difference between those who have a stable, high level of non-contingent self-esteem, and those with low and contingent levels, namely someone with healthy self-esteem recognizes their limitations and expects to learn, grow, and improve over the course of their lifetime. They do not demand the impossible—perfection—from themselves and so will avoid inevitable feelings of failure when that impossible goal is not achieved.

Of course, there can be too much of a good thing. So, before we move on to look at what happens when high levels of self-esteem run out of control, let's sum up the key difference between low and healthy levels of self-esteem with the simple notion that someone with healthy self-esteem respects themselves while someone with low self-esteem is full of self-loathing, self-contempt, and has no respect for themselves.

NARCISSISM AND THE DARK SIDE OF SELF-ESTEEM

Researchers warn there is a dark side of self-esteem and that when it comes to self-worth it is not as simple as thinking more can only be a good thing. This is why, in this book, we are working with the 13 steps I will share with you toward optimum and not just higher levels of self-esteem.

People with high self-esteem who tip over and out of the optimum level can start to show signs of conceit and arrogance and may, researchers say, even demonstrate narcissistic tendencies. This means the sole pursuit of higher self-esteem can come at an unexpected cost to the person chasing this dream, especially if their idea of puffing themselves up is to bring others down to inflate their own standing. When this is the case, then the pursuit of higher levels of self-esteem has become counterproductive and the idea of an optimum level becomes all the more important.

If you have ever had the misfortune to run into someone with narcissistic traits, then you will already know that until you understand what you are dealing with; it can feel as if the world (as you knew it) has turned on its head. Narcissists cannot tolerate even the slightest criticism or any form of negative feedback, however well meaning, so while they may come across, initially, as confident, and with healthy levels of self-esteem, this is an act.

The worst characteristics of a narcissist include having a highly inflated and grandiose view of themselves and their achievements, of their positive traits and competencies and, as a result, of their entitlement. You may be sitting in a fancy restaurant and hear someone with narcissistic tendencies announce: "This is a bit of me. This is my kind of place," as if they have been born with a right to privileges that may be denied to others.

I promise you, you will know if your path has ever crossed with that of a narcissist. You will find yourself feeling confused and befuddled by all the grandiose claims and the excessive need for admiration this person will demonstrate. Hang on, weren't we just reading about the need to be admitted and approved of by others? Who was it that had that character trait?

Interestingly, it wasn't the person with high and healthy self-esteem. It was the description of those telltale signs of poor and low self-esteem, which tells us something very revealing about the narcissist —they may want you to believe that they have high self-value but the truth is very different.

The academic literature on this topic tells us the following:

Narcissists see themselves as the center of the universe; in the mirror, they only see themselves reflected. They see themselves as if they were the only reality worthy of esteem, the rest being mere generators of their supposed grandeur and worth. Narcissists are always talking about their supposed greatness and worth, about their uncommon, marvelous experiences, their extremely interesting projects, about how much they have done to improve in life, and even to help others.

But the research also tells us something else which is just as and perhaps even more revealing because according to studies which look at high levels of self-esteem among normal people and among those with narcissistic tendencies, what we see is that with the narcissist (who is actually faking it), there is a tendency toward aggression and aggressive behavior when they are challenged or criticised and this is not the case among those who have high but genuine self-esteem.

Some researchers have attributed exaggerated levels of self-esteem as being the underlying feature of narcissism but here is another definition of a narcissist from the academic literature which sits fully at odds with the long list of character traits we've just looked at that relate to those with high and healthy levels of self-esteem.

> *"The essential feature of narcissistic personality disorder is a pervasive pattern of grandiosity, need for admiration, a grandiose sense of self-importance, a belief that they are superior, special, or unique."*

HOW EXAGGERATED LEVELS OF SELF-ESTEEM CAN CAUSE SELF-HARMING BEHAVIORS

Researchers who have studied unwise behavior choices among groups identified as having high, but not necessarily healthy, self-esteem have also found this "false" self play a self-justificatory role when it comes to defending choosing harmful behaviors such as drinking, smoking, and having unprotected sex.

In these cases, the high (but not healthy) self-esteem becomes a kind of false shield against the potential negative consequences of these behaviors with a form of self-belief being used to minimize the actual risks to health and to convince the participant that they have some kind of special protection because they are special. In this instance, a false kind of high self-esteem is being used to justify the inconsistencies between the risky behaviors and their positive self-perception.

UNDERSTANDING WOMEN AND SELF-ESTEEM

Although everything in this book applies to both men and women, we have seen how even as early as adolescence, a gap in self-esteem levels between the sexes begins to make itself known and felt. This is why I have targeted the title of this book toward women and why I will, throughout the upcoming chapters and program Steps, put a focus on females where it is needed. Here, I want to end this chapter by touching on some of those additional difficulties facing women whose self-esteem may be shattered and/or vulnerable at best.

For women, it can feel as if there is an ever-present risk of a double assault to our self-worth and to how we really feel about ourselves and our place in the world. As well as being expected to stay young and beautiful forever and to meet someone impossible and idealistic glossy magazine idealization of what beautiful means. We may be subject to abusive experiences which join with those cultural messages to shatter our self-esteem.

Any woman with low self-esteem may feel she has no control over her life and that she is not worth bothering with. She may put herself last on the "to care for" list and be too scared to ask her partner, family, or friends to help her meet her own needs.

If abuse, verbal or physical, has started in childhood (and this applies to both sexes), there may be no self-esteem left to protect leaving the sufferer feeling worthless and not knowing who they really are. Poor self-esteem can cause anxiety and depression and can lead to self-harming because there feels like no other way to release all that pent-up pain and anger.

Relationships can be toxic and troublesome because someone who has a shattered self-esteem does not feel worthy of love and care and will not expect or ask for it. These women may struggle to set boundaries with their partners and their children and because they don't respect themselves, finding parenting difficult because they cannot set limits or demand the respect they deserve.

Worse of all, mothers with low self-esteem risk passing that sense of being worthless and not worth bothering with onto their children. Their daughters may feel the same lack of self-respect and self-worth, and their sons may think all women are prepared to put everyone else's needs first and then expect that from his partner when he has one.

In the workplace too, women with low or shattered self-esteem will put themselves at the back of the promotion queue or even stay out of the limelight for fear of causing offence. They will willingly allow someone else to take the credit for their hard work, will trade on a self-deprecating humour that allows everyone else to feel superior and unthreatened by them, and may never put themselves forward for the projects or promotions that match their hidden talents.

Even with friends, these are the women that find it hard to say no. They end up doing favors for others and going places they don't want to go because it is easier to say yes than to risk causing offence by saying no.

Happily, all this can change and in the next chapter. I will show you how these changes for the better can only happen once you allow yourself to change how you feel about yourself.

IN THE NEXT CHAPTER

- In **Step 2** which follows, I will show you how you can change the way you feel about yourself and begin to move from a low or vulnerable level of self-esteem to a higher level, and from a contingent to a non-contingent one

3

STEP 2 (PART ONE)

CHANGE THE WAY YOU FEEL ABOUT
YOURSELF

We learned in Step 1 that there are some core values that support our feelings of self-worth and our levels of self-esteem. We need to be able to trust our judgement and believe we can make the best decisions for ourselves and our growth. We need to believe, too, that we can overcome those challenges life throws at us, on our path and that when we "fall over" we can get back up again.

When our self-esteem is strong, we know we can make choices that lead to changes in our lives, and we respect ourselves enough to believe we have as much of a right to happiness and respect and love and self-fulfillment as the next person.

But what if you read this and think, well, I'd like to say I believe all that, but deep down, I just don't?

Do not give yourself a hard time if that is the case. Congratulate yourself on two things: one, your honesty in admitting your self-esteem may need a little help and two, for being smart enough to have made it to this second step where I am going to share with you the key things you can train yourself to think and choose to do to fundamentally change how you feel about yourself.

IDENTIFY YOUR TRIGGERS

This is where we turn detective on ourselves. We need to identify those situations/thoughts/people/comments that dent our self-esteem and, if we allow the situation to escalate, can shatter any feelings of self-worth we had.

It would be useful to start a notebook here to write down the triggers you already know adversely affect you.

Here are some prompt words to help you get started. Notice how our triggers can be other people or situations we find ourselves stuck in. Copy these prompt lists into your notebook, if you like, and then rate the degree of triggering you experience with each person/place or event. Use a tick symbol and rate the worst triggers with x5 ticks, moderate triggers with x3 ticks and the things that are not a trigger for you can just leave blank. And of course, add your own unique triggers to the list.

This exercise works whether we are identifying those triggers that make us feel badly/worse about ourselves (lower our self-esteem) and for identifying those that send up spinning the other way and trigger us to over-compensate by showing up with too much self-confidence and an over-inflated sense of our own worth.

It's worth remembering, again, this book is all about finding just the right amount of self-esteem for you to navigate your way to a happier, healthier and more self-fulfilled life.

Possible People Triggers:

- Mom
- Dad
- My brother/sister
- Grandparents
- "Best" friend
- My partner
- My workmate
- The entire "Happy Family" living next door
- The other person in the changing room opposite who looks better in that dress/jacket than me
- A random person on the internet

Possible Place Triggers:

- Your old school
- Your old college
- A place where you were unhappy at work
- Somewhere you often went with an ex partner who has now left you
- Anywhere other people go to enjoy themselves; parks, playgrounds, fun fairs, carnivals, street food festivals

Life Event Triggers:

- Failing at work
- Failing to get your dream job
- Not doing well in your exams
- A parent walking out
- A step-parent walking in
- Major body changes: you think you're not pretty and that this is unfair
- Rejected by someone you fancy dating with
- Husband/Boyfriend left you for someone else

Notice, as you carry out this exercise, just how easy it is to think of endless lists of things that could be possible triggers that lower or even shatter your fragile self-esteem. You could probably fill your notebook with your lists, but once you've got about 15-20 possible triggers across the three different categories, I want you to choose just two triggers from each category and write alongside them what you would say/or did say to yourself when one of these triggers occurs.

Let me give a quick example because this is not a test, it is just meant as an exercise to get you thinking about someone we all prefer to hide away—your Inner Critic—who is the one responsible for giving your self-esteem a nasty little kicking, usually just around the time when what it most needs is a boost!

Let's take the "Best" friend. You may have been surprised to see this person in the Possible People Triggers list, but if you stop and really think about it, there may have been times when your "Best" friend made you feel unworthy of their time and attention. They may not have intended to make you feel that way, but if you ended up feeling you didn't matter to them at that time as much as they mattered to you, then your self-esteem will have been affected.

Here are some "Best" friend examples. Of course, once you start thinking about your own situation you will have more of your own.

Example: You send your best friend a message asking if they want to meet up and hang out? You get no reply or a reply three days later when the time you were suggesting to meet has been and gone.

Now, the focus here is not on your best friend at all. Maybe they had good reason to reply when it was too late to meet, maybe they had an emergency they had to attend to and it has taken this long for the shock to fade and for them to let people know what happened and that they are now ok.

It doesn't matter.

What matters is what you told yourself when your "Best" friend did not reply.

Again, if you are struggling to remember or (more likely) face up to what you said to yourself, here are some things you may have said:

Maybe they have found a new best friend who is so much better than me.
Perhaps they were only ever pretending to like me.
Nobody likes me.
I don't like me.
No wonder nobody wants to be my friend …

I know. Ouch! But the fact is I bet you said something far worse to yourself than the prompt example I've shared here. I bet you piled all the blame of this latest perceived "abandonment" on your own shoulders, telling yourself you never really deserved such a good friend anyway and that the reason nobody likes you is because you are a horrible person and a waste of space.

Try and be as honest as you can when you write in your notebook what you said to yourself when you found yourself mid trigger of a self-esteem self-attack. Because that's what you're doing—attacking yourself—when you go straight to beating yourself up when something doesn't go your way or the way you expected or hoped.

You've barely paused to take a breath let alone consider maybe life and some other event or some other person just got in the way and that yes, things happen which may affect you but that does not mean they are your fault or that they happen because you don't deserve any better.

I have shared the "Best" friend example for your trigger exercise, but you can choose anything from the prompt list or come up with your own example. The "Best" friend, though, is a good example because one of the things we start to see more clearly when we begin to explore our self-esteem/self-attack/possible people triggers, is that sometimes it is the people we least expect who hurt us the most either inadvertently or sometimes, on purpose. And when that happens, we need to be able to really rely on a strong sense of self-esteem to find the resilience to survive those sorts of "close-to-home" attacks.

When we have completed all 13 steps in this book, I will invite you to return to this exercise to remind yourself just how harshly your Inner Critic/voice currently speaks to you. And then I will remind you of something a very good friend once told me which is you wouldn't speak to the dog that way so why would you talk to yourself like that?

I repeat ... ouch!

START ACTIVELY LISTENING

As I said earlier, what matters throughout this second step of this program to find "just the right amount" of self-esteem to carry you through your life is that we start to really pay attention to how we treat ourselves, how we look after ourselves and what we say to ourselves and Active Listening is an important part of that skill.

When we practice Active Listening with another person, we learn to listen to what they are saying by giving their words our full attention and by resisting the very human urge to wish they'd hurry up and finish speaking so we can have our say and respond. Or, worse, we may just get fed up waiting for that time to come and we may just jump in and speak over them.

When you start Active Listening with your inner voice/Inner Critic —whatever you want to call this shadow part of your personality that gets a kick out of telling you you're rubbish and have no intrinsic value—you are going to do the same thing and resist the urge to jump in, until you've heard everything your critic has to throw at you.

The way you do this is to start paying more attention to that voice and by making a commitment to listen to the end instead of pretending there's no negative internal dialogue taking place. Your notebook will come in handy again here because you can write down exactly what the "attack" voice is saying.

Another Active Listening technique is to listen to what someone has just said to you and then to prove you heard every word by repeating, out loud, what they said.

DON'T BELIEVE EVERYTHING YOU THINK

NOTICE NEGATIVE SELF-TALK

At this stage of learning how to change how you feel about yourself and to change it for good, you are working on noticing what your triggers are and what the "voice" says to you when you are challenged. Try to suspend judgement and remain neutral, however bad the voice (and even the words themselves) get.

Remember, this is still part of your detective fact-finding mission. You need to get to know as much as you can about The Suspect before you make an arrest. The Suspect, here, is that part of you running such a negative dialogue and such a strong self-attack program your self-esteem has no chance of surviving intact.

Once you've done the trigger list exercises, keep your notebook close by as you work your way through the upcoming steps in this book but also as you go about your everyday life. If you can, every time you hear an "attack" get the notebook out and write down what words you heard, what was being said about how and, crucially, how it made you feel about yourself.

Do this for a week and you'll understand that whatever those external triggers may be, the voice you need to get onside in order to boost your self-esteem is the one inside your head trying to derail you at every turn.

That voice is not and is never going to be your friend and ally but the good news is, his/her days are numbered ...

CHALLENGE WRONG THINKING

What do I mean when I use the phrase "wrong thinking"? I really just mean those ways of thinking about things that may be factually wrong and which, when analysed, just don't match the facts. You can fall into a habit of wrong thinking and never really realize it until someone else points it out to you. In fact, there's a strong chance you won't even realize you are doing it.

Psychologists and other skilled talk therapists sometimes refer to these thinking patterns as "cognitive distortions" so you can tell from that phrase that something is being distorted meaning something is not being seen or understood the way it should be.

Here are some Wrong Thinking patterns you may have adopted without even realising it. As with every exercise in this book, try to be as honest (and kind) with yourself as you can be. We are not delving into the murkier parts of our brains and personalities in order to beat ourselves with a big stick but to try to understand what's going on subconsciously so that we can then do something positive to make good and healthy changes.

Take a close look at each of these Wrong Thinking patterns and see if you can identify those that best apply to you:

All-or-nothing thinking: You see things are being either all good or all bad. There are no shades of grey, no nuances, no "spaces" where you can think for yourself. It is a pretty brutal view of the world because it leads to self-talk like, "If I don't make this work I am a complete failure and a waste of space."

Generalised thinking: You treat everything as being an "absolute" and leave no room for outliers or things that may not fit the general pattern but still have value. It is as if you take a great big sweeping brush to every issue/challenge/opportunity for original thinking and clear everything away into a single melting pot. An example of generalised thinking would be telling yourself: *"Bad stuff always happens to me."*

Mental filtering: You can only see "negatives" so that's what you think about and dwell on. The fact is this can only lead to a huge distortion of the truth—of an event or of a person—and doesn't leave much room for any of humanity's best qualities like hope and kindness. For example, you may make a mistake on a work project and then tell yourself, "Now everyone will know I'm incompetent and not capable of the job."

Converting positives into negatives: It takes some doing, but you're brilliant at turning anything that is or has been positive into a negative, including your personal and work achievements. For example, you'll tell yourself, "They're only interested in me because nobody else turned up to the event" or "I only did well in that quiz because it was super simple."

Jumping to negative conclusions: You manage to reach a negative conclusion despite the fact there is little or no evidence to support it. Let's use the "Best" friend example again. You didn't think oh, something cropped up and she/he will be in touch when they can, you told yourself, "I never got a reply, so I must have done something to make my friend angry with me." You have absolutely zero evidence that this is true!

Fortune telling: You're projecting to a future—and a negative outcome—that's written in the stars, and which nobody can see. Perhaps you've convinced yourself you're now going to lose your job because you made a mistake at work. You've had a week of sleepless nights yet your boss hasn't said a word or even hinted that you're up for the chop.

Catastrophizing: This is what happens when you start with the fortune telling wrong pattern of thinking. If we stick with the "lost job" example you've probably already "seen" yourself in the queues at the local Food Bank and living in a tent on the streets. Again, you have no evidence. Nothing has happened and nobody has said anything to suggest you are about to lose your livelihood.

Mistaking feelings for facts: You are convinced if you feel a certain way then that must be how something is. For example, you feel like a failure today which means, with this pattern of wrong thinking, you are a failure! Feelings though are not facts.

Magnification/minimisation: Again, a pattern of wrong thinking based not on fact but on distortion. Wrong thinking can help you magnify or minimise a problem; what it won't do is help you to solve one. For example, you will think (and believe): "*My life's not worth living if I don't get into the college I want to go to.*"

Negative self-talk: You don't value yourself, you put yourself down in public and in private, and you tell yourself, repetitively, "I don't deserve any better." This way of wrong thinking is good for distancing yourself from the pain when things go wrong or you lose something you care about but in the long run, it will trip you up and mean you miss out on some of the good stuff that is rightfully yours.

DISARM YOUR INTERNAL CRITIC

Take a deep breath because we are now going to meet your Inner Critic, who is sometimes also called your Pathological Critic and whom I think of as your Super Critic where the word "super" means more critical of you than anyone else in your life!

Before we start to get to know this troubled soul—who is really a shadow part of your own personality—let's take a look at how he/she/they came into being at around the same time you were finding your way in the world.

We'll look at some key therapeutic concepts in this exploration but if you want the shorthand version of what's going on here then it is as follows:

At some point in your life you developed a highly effective defense mechanism who we are now calling your Internal/Inner/Pathological/Super Critic. This part of your personality was given the all-important task of protecting you from the worst that life could throw at you and very likely decided the best form of defence is: attack.

The trouble is, the person your new attack dog, aka Inner Critic, is most likely to attack is: you! And unless we break that unhealthy cycle it is difficult to develop a strong and sustainable level of self-esteem.

The Attack-Dog Cycle Your Inner Critic Just Loves: Difficult/triggering event = blames self = easier in the short term than facing losses/challenges.

Unfortunately, avoiding facing the fact that life is random and that BAD THINGS can and do happen to GOOD PEOPLE becomes a harder choice than facing those facts in the long term because we don't then build the resilience we need to support a healthy and strong level of self-esteem.

You can now see the importance of disarming your Inner Critic (Attack Dog) but how on earth do you go about that? Nobody in their right mind steps toward a snarling dog (and this is how I want you to imagine your Inner Critic); anyone with an ounce of common sense will just avoid eye contact and slip quietly off into the sidelines.

The fact is we need to befriend this Attack Dog and teach him/her/they that there are better ways to protect us and they all start (and stop) with helping us rebuild our self-esteem. You don't go into any kind of battle without first researching and getting to know whatever you can about your adversary and this battle is no different: if you want to defeat your Inner Critic (Attack Dog) you need to understand what drives and motivates him/her/they and change that behavior (your behavior) at its core.

Here, according to psychotherapists, are some of the ways that your Attack Dog (Inner Critic) grew big and strong and got to be the boss of you when you were busy looking the other way or licking your wounds.

HOW YOUR ATTACK DOG GREW BIG & STRONG

- You began to blame yourself for all of the failures of your parents or other primary caregivers to meet your fundamental needs
- You adopted the hostile attitudes other people have shown toward you and started treating yourself with the same degree of hostility
- You began comparing yourself unfavorably to others

- You decided you could only win the praise or approval of others through great achievements or demonstrating you are perfect
- You realized you could protect yourself by criticizing yourself before anyone else could
- You started to limit your life experiences and stop yourself from taking resilience-building and healthy risks because you felt you'd never achieve the goals you wanted to set for yourself
- You became convinced that if you set a goal but failed to achieve that desired outcome, your life would collapse and catastrophe would reign

I promised we'd learn how to disarm your Inner Critic and to do that we are going to muster all our intelligence and skills because what we are really going to do is outwit the Attack Dog. You don't want to destroy this "gate-keeper" because once properly trained he/she/they can do an important job in helping you to stand up for yourself when you are challenged but first, we need to retrain them so the focus turns outwards and is not directed at you.

Self-hate and loathing, as I've explained, can feel easier and most comfortable than having to face unkindness/spite or even just the randomness of life in the outside world but self-hate destroys self-esteem and so we need to gather our wits and disarm our Inner Critic without drawing blood!

Here are the key strategies we'll rely on to retrain our Attack Dog and create a healthier relationship with the part of our persona that is allowed to question what we are doing and why, but which we cannot allow to prevent us from celebrating what is good in our lives and moving forward positively in our lives.

THE SIX KEY STRATEGIES FOR DISARMING YOUR INNER CRITIC

1. Defuse
2. Dispute
3. Dialog
4. Displace
5. Deepen
6. Distance

Let's look at each of these so that when we feel ready to start retraining our Inner Critic, we have all the skills and understanding of why he/she/they behave the way they do which means we can retrain them with confidence.

Defuse

This is a psychological term taken from the school of Acceptance Commitment Therapy (ACT) which simply means: we observe what happens to us without being swept away on a tide of negative reactions. Another way to think about this is to realize that you can decide to stay neutral and not dive into the maelstrom. Negative thoughts only intensify painful feelings and then we end up making decisions that don't reflect our core values or best interests but are a knee-jerk reaction to something bad happening. The defusing technique teaches us (and our Attack Dog) that a thought is not the same as a reality!

Staying neutral will reassure your Attack Dog and let him/her/they know it is ok to stand down; you are safe and nothing catastrophic is about to happen.

Dispute

Another way to disarm your Inner Critic is to just respond to negative thoughts about yourself by asking two words: *Says who?* This technique, taken from the school of Cognitive Therapy (CT), teaches us to question negative and wrongful thinking by asking for rationale and evidence. Of course there won't be any evidence, and so this is a great way to disarm your Inner Critic. You could also just say, ok, I hear what you are saying but before I take any action, I need you to prove it to me. He/she/they can't, so who wins? You do.

Disputing simply means questioning whether an assertion is fact. Ask your Attack Dog to show you the proof, and they'll probably slide away to play with their peanut-butter filled Kong toy.

(Compassionate) Dialog

This technique comes from the school of thought that maintains that the different parts of the Self can talk to each other and, just as importantly, each part—including the Inner Critic (Attack Dog)—is positively motivated to help not harm you. Dialoging is a key strategic part of a psychological framework known as Internal Family Systems (IFS), which takes the view that the Self can remain composed throughout "dialoguing" with other parts of the personality and thanks to this composure, can engage compassionately, even with the Inner Critic.

The Self can have an intelligent and compassionate conversation with the Inner Critic (Attack Dog) and explain that while he/she/they mean well, there is no need to place blame on the Self as a form of defense. Together, the Self and the Inner Critic can face whatever life throws their way. You can think of this as the Self giving the Inner Critic much-needed therapy and a place to vent.

. . .

Displace

We touched on this technique a little earlier in this chapter when I shared the story of a friend who once told me you wouldn't speak to your dog that way. She meant the way the Inner Critic speaks to us. And she's right—you wouldn't speak to the family pet, someone you love, or a young child in such harsh tones, and acknowledging that is the first step in stopping speaking with such a lack of compassion to yourself. Displacement goes one clever step further and invites you to imagine someone who has been kind to you in the past, someone you know has your best interests at heart. You then simply displace the Inner Critic (Attack Dog) with the voice of this kinder soul.

Place both your hands over your heart. Close your eyes, take a deep breath and bring to mind the voice of this "Kind Person" saying something compassionate to you. Really listen to their tone and feel the love they have toward you. You won't even notice the Attack Dog slope away to take a snooze by the fireside. He/she/they can now rest in the knowledge you are in good and safe and protective hands.

Deepen

This technique comes from the Hakomi Method of Psychotherapy which is similar to better-known mindfulness practices. It serves to actually strengthen (deepen) your relationship with and understanding of your Inner Critic as a way of finally disarming him/her/them. And the way you deepen this relationship is to go back, in your mind, to when your Inner Critic was starting out (and the Attack Dog was just a puppy) and remembering what happened to you to trigger such strong responses in them.

Imagine yourself sitting on a picnic blanket on top of a hill on summer's day with your faithful Inner Critic (Attack Dog) by your side. See yourself taking hold of their hand—or if you are going with the idea of the Attack Dog placing your hand gently on their head—and in your mind revisit, together, a trauma from your childhood that left you feeling your world might end. Allow yourself to become upset and know you are in the imaginary realms; this is not happening all over again. When you come out of this state, remind yourself and your Inner Critic that both of you got it wrong. Yes, it was a trauma but no, your world did not end.

If you feel this type of inner "feeling" work resonates with you and you have the resources, you can find a therapist who will also work safely with you to disarm that Inner Critic.

Distance

You may have noticed by now that as soon as you started to "distance" yourself from that negative inner voice, "it" started losing some of its power over you. There are schools of thought that urge us to set out to destroy the Inner Critic or Attack Dog entirely, but I don't subscribe to these because it is my belief, as we saw in the section on Dialoguing, that the Inner Critic (Attack Dog) started out life thinking they were helping you. And so all that has happened is that their defensive and protective behaviors have gotten out of hand over the years.

Now you're starting to learn how to retrain those internal voices so that they stop automatically attacking you—and you stop believing every word they say—you will already feel you've taken an important step back.

Sometimes, it is hard to make a good assessment of a situation and what's needed to adjust and move forward when we are right in the middle of it and so this step back is a really important part of changing the voices we listen to.

That's what we are moving on to now: some thoughts about replacing the Inner Critic and the negative thinking with healthier and more positive voices and outcomes. Before we do that, take a moment to enjoy your new view from here—with here being a step or two back and out of the maelstrom of negative thoughts and feelings about yourself!

NOTICE THE GOOD STUFF

This is such an obvious but often overlooked way of replacing what you don't want with what you do want. For me, it's like imagining you decide you want to get healthy and stay healthy so you go shopping and come home with health-boosting superfoods, nuts, seeds, green leafy veg, fruit juice, and all sorts of delicious but healthy treats. It will feel a bit strange starting this new healthy eating plan but your body (and your mind and spirit) are going to love you for taking such good care of them.

Your skin will glow, you'll have more energy and you'll be more than a match for any internal negative voices or commentary!

First though, you need to make space in the fridge and the store cupboards for all this healthy superfood and to do that you probably have to ditch the old processed, unhealthy snacks, and cheat meals.

I'm sharing the "clear the store cupboard and fridge" metaphor with you because I want you to imagine that you are doing the same to your mind when you start to swap the negative narrative for a more positive one.

I'm going to share some ideas here for ways you can change the narrative and each time you think or feel something good about yourself, I want you to make "space" for that thought or feeling by ditching one of the old more critical ideas you were holding on to. Remember, we're not putting the Inner Critic/Attack Dog down; we are just retraining him/her/them.

BRING ON THE GOOD THINGS!

You're going to need your notebook again because this is a part of the book where you do the work, and I applaud your efforts from the sidelines.

I'm going to ask you to do a number of tasks that serve to celebrate who you really are, what you have achieved so far, and when you read back the list, I want you to imagine my voice in your ear complimenting you on what a wonderful person you are!

Celebrate your successes: No matter how small or insignificant you think they are (go away Inner Critic!) take some time to notice what you did well and praise yourself. If you are struggling to find things you've done well over the past week or month or even year, you are allowed to include past successes. Focus on the "small wins" and use these feelings of success as a springboard.

Accept compliments: When did someone last pay you a compliment? What did they say? Write it down in your notebook and make yourself read it out loud. Next time you start feeling low or doubting you are worthy of love or praise or attention, go back to this page in your notebook and read the complement out loud again.

If you're chilling with friends and feel comfortable in doing so, ask them what they like about you: You can explain you are doing some "inner" work this week and say as little or as much as you like about the fact that you're working on being kinder to yourself/building your self-esteem. Ask people what they like about you. It's likely that they see you differently to how you see yourself. This is a very revealing exercise and you'll be surprised by just how differently your friends or family see you and think about you compared with the way you (and your Inner Critic) have been seeing you.

Don't focus on the negatives: If someone says something unhelpful or unkind, you and your Inner Critic will want to focus solely on that and then ignore anything positive that may have been said or have happened to you. Resist this urge. We want to retrain the Inner Critic/Attack Dog not keep feeding them the wrong ideas.

Write a list of everything you like about yourself: This is no time to be shy or modest. Write the list ... you can include character traits, skills or experience, beliefs or causes that matter to you and things you enjoy doing. You can ask other people for suggestions too. Take a look at your CV if you have one; it will remind you of the skills and experiences you've picked up in your work and in life. It will be difficult to walk away from this exercise without a new sense of your own unique value as a person.

SET NEW SELF-BELIEFS

Setting new core beliefs about yourself follows naturally on from all the work we've done so far in this important Step 2; we've learned what we can do to retrain our Inner Critic/Attack Dog and we've got a list (in our notebook) of things we like about ourselves, things other people like about us, and things we've achieved that we should be celebrating.

So here then are some strategies which will help you get started in setting a series of new self-beliefs and core values—all designed to help you achieve a strong and healthy level of self-esteem and just the right amount: not too much and not too little.

Practice using "hopeful" thoughts: Things may not always go the way we expect or want, but that doesn't mean there is no value in them. If you are facing a tough situation at work, home, or in your relationships, see this as an opportunity to begin establishing new beliefs, starting with making hopeful statements. Yes, you may be dreading what is looming, but tell yourself, "*I know it will be tough but hopefully I can handle this.*" Don't ever underestimate the power of hope and the usefulness of the word "hopefully" when facing a challenge.

Learn to forgive yourself: We saw earlier in this chapter how aiming for "perfection" is a defense mechanism that only serves to feed the hungry Inner Critic/Attack Dog. Nobody is perfect, and that includes you! Everyone makes mistakes—and that includes you! What you need to learn is that a mistake does not determine who you are as a person. It is an isolated moment in time. Get the Self to sit down with the Inner Critic/Attack Dog and explain that whilst it is true, you made a genuine mistake—that does not mean you are a bad person.

Avoid the shoulda/coulda/woulda trap: Hindsight is a wonderful thing, as long as you don't use it to beat yourself up. If you use words like "Should" and "Could" and "Must," you are being the kind of unreasonably demanding person most of us would avoid in real life. Eliminating these words from the internal dialogue will help reshape more reasonable expectations of yourself (and others). It sounds like a small step, but try it because it is one that pays quick dividends in terms of how you feel about yourself and rate yourself. As you're ditching these "demand" words, remind yourself that most of us do the best we can in any given situation with whatever information we have at that time. And NOBODY IS PERFECT!

P is for positives: Choose one day this week to focus only on the positives. Notice those areas of your life that are working well for you. Notice the skills you've acquired when you've had to deal with more challenging people/situations/triggers. P is also for Pat on the Back. Give yourself one.

It's a learning curve: And sometimes a very steep one! If you have had something bad happen to you or around you in recent times, try to think about how it could have been avoided. Was there anything you could have done differently? If not, move on. This was outside your control. If you can see, though, that you could have done something differently that would have led to a more positive outcome, then you've learned something and taken another step up the Learning Curve. Well done!

What did you learn?: If you now know you could have done something differently and saved yourself a negative experience, think about what you would do differently in the exact same circumstance. Write it down. Acknowledge it. Be grateful for this new information.

Rename negative thoughts: We've used the terms negative thoughts and negative thinking in this chapter, so we can recognize those thoughts/ideas and internal narratives that are tripping us up and damaging our self-esteem, but what do you think would happen if you stopped calling them "negative" and instead recognized them as alarm bells or warning signals that are simply asking you to find new, healthier patterns of thoughts and behaviors. Can you see how just by renaming something we can turn3 it from an adversary to a friend? Genius … And when these old thought patterns do intrude, ask yourself, *"What can I think and do to make all of this less stressful for me?"*

Encourage yourself: Give credit where credit is due. If you make positive changes, give yourself credit for this. If something goes wrong and, instead of beating yourself up, you remember to get "Self" to sit down with Inner Critic (Attack Dog) and explain this, doesn't make you useless/a waste of space/someone not worth bothering with/unlovable/unreliable or incapable of achieving the goals you share with them? Remember, they are on your side really. Then, please also remember to congratulate yourself (and them) because you have just more than ably demonstrated a brand new self-belief and healthier pattern of behavior.

IN THE NEXT CHAPTER

- Now you know more about how to silence your Inner Critic/Attack Dog and win them over to the side which knows you're worthy of a good and happy life, we will move on to Step 3 of our program and learn more about retraining the brain to stop all negative self-talk for good

4

STEP 2 (PART TWO)

RETRAINING THE BRAIN TO NOTICE AND REMEMBER THE GOOD STUFF

THE MIRACLES GOING ON INSIDE YOUR HEAD

Did you know that you can use your mind to change your brain to change your mind?

Think about that.

If we want to make real and lasting changes, then we need to make them where it counts—in our amazing brains. And so to motivate you to want to do that, in this chapter, we're going to look at the science behind making positive and lasting changes to the brain—by which I mean, to the way we think about ourselves.

The brain is a complex and astonishingly brilliant organ. Did you know it is made up of 1.1 trillion cells? No wonder then that it is quite likely we will never know all its secrets or everything about how it works to shape our thinking, who we are and how we respond to life. But the way I see it, there is a whole lot of value in finding out what we know so far and what questions brain researchers and psychologists concerned with self-esteem are now asking themselves and each other.

Neuroanatomy is the study of the anatomy of the brain. Neuro-science is the study of the function of your brain which scientists admit could just be the most amazingly complex object in the universe! That's right. That 3lb mass of tofu-textured soft tissue that you carry around on the inside of your protective skulls is a miracle of nature and science (and divinity, if you are a person of faith).

Your brain is always "on", and whilst you will never even be aware of most of its functioning, you are aware (or can be) of its slower processes which happen to be those processes that include your thoughts and feelings.

THINKING ABOUT THINKING ...

If you closed your eyes and spent a minute or two thinking about a thought, what would that look like to you? It may be you "see" in your "mind's eye" a train rushing past or an arrow heading straight for the bull's-eye on the archery board. It is likely, when you think about thinking, you imagine something fast-moving and something with a destination from (a) to (b) which requires rapid movement.

How about feelings?

Close your eyes and imagine feeling sad for a moment. What comes to mind (use your powers of imagination here) when you think about feeling sad? You may "see" a color or hear a sad song. You may see the petals falling from a dying rose.

You may, again, see something in transition but this time something moving away from you and forever lost to you. Which creates a feeling that stays with you: a feeling of sadness.

Perhaps your sad feelings feel heavy. Maybe they are buried under a pile of stones because in truth, you don't want to feel this way, and that's fine because who does? Or maybe when I ask you to imagine a feeling of sadness as a function of brain activity, you can see, in your mind's eye, tiny droplets of water running down a windowpane, as if the whole world were crying with you.

The reason I'm asking you to think about thinking for a moment is so you can experience your thoughts, rather than them being something that you may feel you have no control over. It's true that a thought, especially a negative one, may pop unbidden into your head, but that does not mean you have to go with it. You don't have to believe it. You don't have to engage with it. You don't even have to "own" it because if it is a thought that is negative about or toward you, then it probably never even came from you in the first place but from someone else who was careless about what they said around you, or even deliberately hurtful.

Try it for yourself now.

Think of something horrible to say to yourself about yourself. And as soon as you have had that thought, send it on its way. Just imagine putting it on a train with a one-way ticket and waving it off from the platform.

The thought has gone. It is history now. You are not.

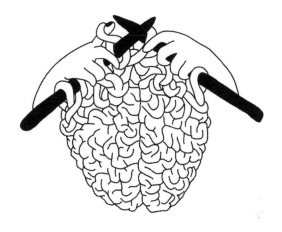

THE FEMALE BRAIN

It turns out there is a specific area of your brain that has been given the all-important task of negative thinking, and guess what? Not only has this part of the brain been shown to be larger in women than in men, but there is a serious evolutionary reason for this discrepancy.

Louann Brizendine, MD, is an American-trained neuropsychiatrist and the author of a book called *The Female Brain*. She has spent her career studying brain differences between the sexes and says the reason women react more strongly to criticism and negative feedback than men is because this part of their brain is larger.

"It is judgemental," she says. "It is the part of the brain that monitors every social interaction you have, and so is the part that tells you you're too fat or too old and it goes on red alert when the feedback you are getting from others isn't going so well."

Women's brains have also developed with a more acute sensitivity to the emotions of others than the brains of men, and the key reason for these differences, says Brizendine, is that women have been built to be able to "read" and immediately respond to the needs of a nonverbal infant. In other words, you need to be able to monitor, assess, and read the clues your baby gives so you can work out whether to change a nappy or offer a bottle. And this, says Dr. Brizendine, can be a good thing (good for the baby that needs your care and attention) and a bad thing (bad for maintaining healthy self-esteem when you are super sensitive to criticism).

And there are other biological reasons women are more sensitive to emotional nuance which have nothing to do with child rearing because according to Dr. Brizendine, how you interpret feedback from others will also depend on where you are in your menstrual cycle and the hormone surges that regulate ovulation and menstruation.

"Some days, the feedback will reinforce your self-confidence and on other days, the exact same feedback will destroy you," she says.

Dr. Brizendine has been studying how the menstrual hormone surges can affect self-esteem ever since medical school when she says she became fascinated about why teenage girls would come to believe bad things about themselves.

"There's something about the menstrual cycle that puts your emotional self in a bad light at least for a few days every month. About 90 percent of women feel some kind of increased emotionality two to four days before their period starts, where they're crying over dog food commercials. I wanted to get a message to girls who are slipping down some slippery slope and get a safety net under them," she says. (Ball, 2019)

ANOTHER REASON WE ONLY HEAR (AND REMEMBER) THE BAD STUFF

We've seen how external events can damage someone's self-esteem, but psychologists also understand that as we develop from childhood to adulthood, we begin to judge ourselves according to three distinct impressions or understandings we have of who we are and how we value ourselves.

These three "ideas" are just that—ideas that we all carry around inside our heads—which are a direct result of our thoughts about:

(i) who we really are

(ii) who we really want to be

(iii) who we dread becoming or being.

These are known as the Real Self, the Ideal Self and the Dreaded Self.

Tune in for a moment to this concept and see if you can identify your own Real Self, Ideal Self, and Dreaded Self.

Now think about the kinds of words we might use to describe each of these three versions of you. For example, you may say to yourself:

- My Real Self is good/bad/a mix of the two; just like everyone else
- My Ideal Self is perfect and that's why people love him/her/them
- My Dreaded Self is horrible and that's why everyone hates him/her/them

Which of these three "Selves" is your favorite? Which one would you choose to be all of the time if someone gave you the choice? Most of us will choose the Ideal Self—the perfect being who, in reality, does not exist. If this is the "Self" you want to be, all of the time, then you are setting yourself up for failure and inviting self-criticism and negative self-talk which will, in turn, lower your self-esteem and how you think about yourself because nobody can live up to an ideal. Not you, not me, and not the most perfect person on the planet.

As we mature and start to compare ourselves and our achievements against those of others, the Dreaded Self starts to play a bigger role and can even overshadow both the Real Self and the Ideal Self.

We may start to worry that the Dreaded Self is who we are destined to become, and that once that happens, nobody will want to be around us, let alone love us.

Researchers report that self-esteem takes a serious battering and declines fast when we start believing we are on the way to becoming this Dreaded Self, so we need to nip this kind of negative thinking in the bud before the damage is done.

The truth is you are neither your Ideal nor your Dreaded Self. These are both just thoughts and fears you are projecting onto yourself.

The truth is, you are your Real Self; a person who is a perfectly normal mix of good and sometimes not so good: a person who sometimes succeeds and sometimes fails. A person who does not have to be or become perfect for others to value and love them. A person who does not have to be or become perfect for them to love and value themselves.

POSITIVE BRAIN CHANGE—GROWING THE GOOD STUFF

The good news is that we can learn to deliberately stimulate those parts of the brain that trigger positive thinking about ourselves regardless of what other people are saying about or to us, and if we can learn to do that, then we can change our thinking to change our minds about how we feel about ourselves.

Everything you think, feel, say, do, and believe about yourself is controlled by one thing: your brain. So, if you can take charge of that, you can take charge of your self-esteem.

Imagine a day where 10 different things happen to you—these can be events or just comments someone else makes. This can be a leisure day at home, or a hardworking day at work, or college, or even school. So, nine of these 10 things are really positive. They make you feel good about yourself. They leave you feeling happy. But one of these comments is negative. It may be about your appearance, or something you said or misunderstood, or relate to your performance during a particular task. Or it may be a group of friends forgot to tell you they were meeting for lunch, leaving you feeling left out and hurt.

Of the 10 things that happen to you during this imaginary day—nine positive things and one negative—which one do you remember?

And not only which one do you remember but how long do you obsess over it for?

Brain scientists now know the brain has what they call a "negativity" bias. In other words, your biology will favor you remembering the one negative thing that happened. So, when we think about growing and finding the good stuff, we need to try extra hard because we have to overcome that built-in bias which is leftover from the days when our very survival depended on being able to make a fast assessment of our physical safety and run if danger was heading our way.

We are, biologically, predisposed to look for bad news, and therefore all of us have a tendency to over-focus on it, but, as we saw earlier in this chapter, women even more so than men!

If your brain was simply an app on your smartphone, then this negativity bias would simply be an annoying "bug" that the developers would eventually get around to fixing. You'd be able to download an update and off you would go: problem fixed.

Brain researcher, Rick Hanson PhD, stresses just how strong the bias toward storing and remembering negative experiences is when he says: "Most positive and beneficial experiences simply wash through our brains, like water through a sieve."

According to Rick, the primary way to grow as a person is to gather all the good experiences we can in order to store them in the brain and change its neural structure for good to give us the internal resources we will need to enjoy a happy life.

When he talks about "the good stuff" Rick, who is also the author of a book called *Buddha's Brain*, is talking about a long list of positive experiences including:

Rick's List

- Resilience
- Confidence
- Self-confidence
- Happiness
- Determination
- Compassion
- Self-compassion
- Gratitude

The key, he says, is to take these experiences and turn them into lasting changes to the neural network and coding in the brain because otherwise, they are of no lasting value. They don't, he says, make you psychologically stronger or help you grow as a person unless you find a way to change the brain so they can be stored as positive resources for you to draw on.

It all sounds great, but how do we do that? How do we tip the balance for the brain to favor and store our more positive experiences, and how do we change the brain in order to change our minds and, by changing our minds, find our way to a stable, lasting, and non-contingent form of self-esteem?

The answer lies in the discovery that our brains are not fixed—but change (and thus changes our minds) depending on how we stimulate them and which parts we stimulate.

This is the new science of neuroplasticity which proves that as the brain changes, so the mind (and what you think, including what you think about yourself) changes too.

And then, as the mind changes, the brain changes as well, both in temporary and more lasting ways. And so, when it comes to self-esteem, we already know what we are after are positive changes that stick so, without getting too deep into the brain science, let's see how we might go about achieving this goal.

POSITIVE NEURAL PLASTICITY

Scientists have discovered that the portion of the brain that is more closely linked with positivity and positive experiences is the left front section. This is called the left prefrontal cortex and it is this part of the brain that mind researchers have discovered plays a key role in controlling negative emotions. This, if you think about it, is a way of looking at the issue from the other side; if you put the brakes on the negative, then you allow for more of the positive.

Mental activity (thinking/feeling) has been shown to produce changes in neural activity (brain functioning.) For example, people practising gratitude produce more of the feel-good brain chemicals (neurotransmitters) which enliven the mind and boost feelings of being in a good mood and enjoying overall well-being. This isn't a case of wishful thinking and wouldn't that be great ... Researchers have monitored the brains of people meditating on gratitude, for example, and this is what they find.

Another way to think of this, especially when it comes to making lasting brain changes, is to understand that whatever you allow to flow through your mind—information that the brain will then process and store—will be what sculpts your brain and shapes its activities.

But how do these changes become lasting?

We can achieve lasting changes because the information that flows into the brain will set off patterns of neural firing. What people like Rick and other researchers mean when they say "neurons that fire together wire together" is that it is these patterns that create the changes to neural structure that will be lasting changes.

You have already experienced this for yourself. Think of something, some activity, that you know you are good at. It could be a specific sport, or art, or music, or anything that you enjoy and engage in on a regular basis. Now, ask yourself this: were you born good at this activity? Of course not. You learned the skills and then, over time, honed them so that now you are competent and maybe even brilliant at it. This is because what was happening as you practised and honed these skills is that you created new neural pathways in your brain which you reinforced every time you practised and which became a lasting part of your own neural networks.

Your brain is also designed to favor its "busy" regions—so those neural networks and pathways you stimulate when, for example, you play a musical instrument or take part in your favorite sport, get more blood than other regions. Busy regions also begin to stitch together to create newer pathways and networks which, if you think about it, might as well be positive and beneficial to you!

Busy regions of the brain get stronger. They get more receptive. They start building more synapses so that new neurons can all reach each other to create new networks. If this all sounds ingenious, then that is because it is. We started this chapter talking about the miracles going on inside your head, and now you can begin to visualize some of them yourself.

In a study of the brains of London taxi drivers, brain researchers discovered that the part of the brain involved in memory and spatial awareness has become visibly thicker after the drivers complete their training, which includes memorizing the maze and network of London streets so they don't have to rely on sat nav or even an old fashioned map. They know their way around and the short cuts they can take if there are roadblocks or delays caused by an accident because they have spent hours training the brain to memorize all the routes and all the alternatives.

Those London taxi drivers who studied so hard to pass the exam, known as "The Knowledge", would not have known what brain researchers have now discovered which is this: you really can use the mind to change the brain to change the mind for the better.

This is known as self-directed neuroplasticity, and it will be a big part of what we will be going on to learn to do through the various steps of this program in order to create not only an optimum level of self-esteem for you but one that will last.

And the key to success once we embark on self-directed neuroplasticity lies in the controlled use of attention. In other words, we can only direct these brain changes if we focus and concentrate on paying attention to the information that will flow into the mind to help us achieve them.

FINDING THE GOOD STUFF IN THE WORLD

One way in which you can start this process of self-directed neuro-plasticity—making positive and lasting brain changes that will create positive and lasting changes to the mind and what you think about yourself—is by learning to pay more attention to the things you give your attention to.

Imagine that every day when you wake up, you wake up with a big bright light beaming from the middle of your forehead onto whatever you choose to look at or notice during that day. This is such a powerful (imaginary) light that it would blind anyone who tried to look directly at it so you need to be careful where you shine this light and make sure you are only using it when it is safe to do so.

In this imaginary scene, the bright light represents your attention.

This may sound odd, but your intent (what you set your mind to do or think about) and your attention are two of the most powerful resources you have at your disposal, so dust them off and start using them to bring more positivity and positive experiences into your life.

Here is a little exercise you can try to get you started.

The next time you step out of your home, imagine you are turning this bright light on so you can really see anything you shine it on.

- You are going to spend the whole day noticing positive things
- Is the sun shining? Does sunshine make you feel happy? If the answer is yes then this counts as something positive happening on this day
- Did your ride to school/college/work show up bang on time so you weren't waiting around? If yes, then this is another positive
- Did you get a WhatsApp message with a comedy sketch video that made you laugh out loud? Two positives there:

(i) someone was thinking about you and wanted to share something they knew you would find funny. This is someone who cares for and about you. (ii) Something made you laugh. Out loud

- Did you see someone helping someone else with their shopping or any other act of kindness? Yup, that's a positive

FINDING THE GOOD STUFF IN YOU

For this exercise, you are going to turn that bright light—your attention—inwards, and instead of shining it out on all the good stuff going on in the outside world, you are going to spend a part of every day from now on shining it on some good things about you.

The Real Self you, not the Ideal Self or the Dreaded Self, neither of which we now know even exist.

When you wake up tomorrow morning, switch your light on, turn it (in your imagination) to shine inside your head and find one thing you like about you or something you did or do.

Just one thing. This does not have to be earth-shattering or Nobel prize-winning, but it will be something that makes you feel valued by someone very important: the Real Self you.

- Did you complete a difficult task at school, or college, or work, one you felt like quitting but didn't? If so, that's a positive. You showed determination (which is on Rick's list of positive resources), so make a mental note of that positive experience and start your day feeling proud of yourself
- Perhaps you went out of your way to help a friend who was feeling a bit down and in need of cheering up. If so, big tick, you showed compassion, another of the resources on Rick's list
- Maybe you had a small win on a scratch card or the lottery and so can treat yourself to something delicious for dinner tonight. Win! That's a positive. Something good happened which made you feel happy, yet another resource on the list

These are baby steps and you will have your own examples of positive experiences once you start to shine the bright light of your focused attention on them. There are no rights or wrongs to chastise yourself with, if something felt positive to you and led to one of the feelings on Rick's list then that is a positive experience you can think about, having had the experience, and allow the memory of it to flow into your mind.

Congratulations: You've just taken your first baby step in self-directed positive neuroplasticity!

IN THE NEXT CHAPTER

- We will look at why finding "Real You" is important before we take more steps in finding our own optimum level of self-esteem

5

FIND YOUR REAL SELF

I n this chapter, I am going to show you how you can recover your self-esteem when it has gone into decline. We will look at the theories, explore what the scientists say, and try a few simple exercises so we can begin to tell the difference between the things that damage our self-esteem (which we have already explored) and those that boost it. But the main focus of this chapter will be on getting to know, and like, the Real You, not the idealised "perfect" you or, worse, the "dreaded" you, both of which are figments of your imagination and fears.

CHANGING THE STORY YOU TELL YOURSELF ABOUT YOU

Working with Real You calls for honesty and kindness. There may be parts about yourself you don't like and try hard to hide from others for fear of negative feedback and criticism. You don't need to worry about that here because the only people who will be in the room will be Real You and Real Me and my only interest is in sharing everything I have studied and learned about self-esteem so that, together, we can work on boosting and supporting yours.

Let's start with the idea of being kinder to yourself. If I was sitting opposite you right now and asked you to share one mean thing you have said or thought about yourself in the last 24 hours, what would that be?

- Have you called yourself fat?
- Have you told yourself you don't deserve any of the "good stuff" life has to offer?
- Have you blamed yourself when things have gone wrong, including things in the external world that you know you have absolutely no control over?
- Have you imagined everyone has life figured out except you, and that you are doomed to failure?

If you have answered "yes" to any of these, then you have been very unkind. To yourself. Would you call your best friend fat? Would you tell someone else it is always their fault when things go awry in their lives? Would you even dream of telling another person—especially someone you care about—they are doomed to failure? No, of course not.

I want you to think too about the tone of voice you used when you spoke to yourself in this way. Were you using soft and loving tones or did your voice, in your head, sound harsh, critical, and impatient with you? Imagine now I was handing you a small kitten or a puppy to hold. What tone of voice would you use when you pet a small, defenceless animal? I bet it would not be a harsh one.

I am not comparing you to a small and defenceless creature. I am just using this as an example to get you to think not only about the words you use when you speak to yourself but how you say them and how harsh all that negative scolding will sound.

Now that you know how to recognize it you also know how to stop it. Instantly. As soon as it starts up and as soon as you hear it. Remember how we learned in the last chapter that whatever flows into the mind can affect the brain and how the brain, in turn, then affects the mind and what we think.

Next time something negative creeps into your self-talk, kick it out by replacing it with a different thought. You can choose what type of thought but if you are struggling, here are some examples.

You Hear (In Your Head)

You are rubbish
That was your fault
Your always mess things up
Everyone hates you
If you were thin you'd win
You will mess this up

You Say (Out Loud)

Every human being is a miracle
I did my best, but I can't control the outcome
I will learn (and grow) from my mistakes
The people who love me won't agree with that
Judging people by their appearance is shallow
I didn't mess it up last time

What I want to demonstrate with this exercise is that you may not feel you can control those critical thoughts that come into your head and feed into that cycle of being unkind to yourself. You can instead, break the cycle and change the pattern by responding with a positive statement about yourself: not some imagined self but the Real You.

This is always the first step in changing how we think and feel about ourselves but it only works if we are honest. If you are really mean to yourself, be honest and admit that and then we can set about changing it.

This little exercise also shows us how one of the sources we can draw on to level up and improve our self-esteem lies within us, and the choices we make about the "story" we tell ourselves, but there are also external sources we can look to in order to change how we feel about ourselves and to help us see we are valued, loved, and worthy, just the way we are.

EXTERNAL SOURCES OF SELF-ESTEEM

Psychologists now recognize self-esteem as something that is on equal footing in importance in your life with those other things that will shape your life choices and experiences, namely your personality and identity. And with the changes in society that place the "Self" right at the heart of those experiences (you need only look to social media and selfies for evidence of this change). There are those that now believe self-esteem has never been more important as something for us to understand and think about, especially when we think about how to have more of it.

For all of us, our self-esteem says something to others and ourselves about who we are (Real You), how we live our lives, and what is unique about self-esteem is that it shapes our responses to whatever is going on in our lives, both negative and positive.

People with stable and optimally healthy levels of self-esteem suffer less of the following:

Guilt

Bitterness

Hostility

Shame

Social Anxiety

Embarrassment

Anger

Depression

Loneliness

Just look at that list which is depressing, in and of itself. Nobody wants to wake up in the morning in the grip of any of those emotions, and ironically, those whose self-esteem is already low don't need a double dose of shame, or guilt, or loneliness, or anxiety to push their self-worth even lower. At its best, low self-esteem will lead to becoming socially isolated as a way of protecting yourself from the risk of having these difficult feelings, and at worst, it can result in outright human misery.

Imagine then how much better you would feel, how much happier your experience of life, and your resilience to the challenges that come your way would be if you could have a list that was the positive and polar opposite to the one above. Wouldn't it be worth changing the way you think about yourself in order to get more of what's on that list? More of the things that will help you flourish and thrive?

Let's start that now by looking at the special science that aims to show us how to improve the quality of our lives by studying what works to make people happier, healthier, and more content. This science is what people now call Positive Psychology.

WHAT IS POSITIVE PSYCHOLOGY?

The easiest way to think about positive psychology is to think of it as being the study of the things that make life worth living.

Before we dig deeper into that idea, take a moment or two to list the things that you believe make YOUR life worth living. If you have a pen and a journal to hand, write them down or make a Note on your smartphone.

If you are struggling to get started, here are 10 keyword "prompts" to get you thinking about what makes a life worth living;

- Family
- Friends
- Love
- Meaningful work
- Helping others
- Looking after a child
- Looking after a pet
- Being exposed to different cultures through travel
- Learning new skills through study
- Listening to music/dancing/enjoying art/making music/making art

Make your own list, there are no rights or wrongs, all that is important is that it is a list that reflects what gets you up and out of bed in the morning. Now, whittle this list down to your Top 3 Picks. Choose just three of these things that give your life meaning and make it feel worthwhile.

I suspect that in some small (or maybe even big) way, you already feel a little bit better than you did before you wrote your list. Something happened as you allowed these positive thoughts to flow through your mind and out through your fingers to your pen or the phone keyboard which made you feel just a little bit better about yourself. Maybe you always felt good. Maybe you felt nothing much at all. Just take a quick moment to enjoy this feeling because this is what self-esteem feels like.

Positive psychology is a relatively new field of study which was kick-started in 1998 when psychologist and self-help author Martin Seligman chose it as the theme for his term as President of the American Psychological Society. It puts its emphasis on happiness, well-being, and positivity and so is a strong reaction against those past practices in psychology that focused on mental illness and maladaptive behaviors and negative thinking.

Positive psychology focuses on *"eudaimonia"* which is an Ancient Greek term for "the good life." It is concerned with all those things that contribute most to a life that is well-lived, and meaningful, and clinicians practising in this field will often use the terms "subjective well-being" and "happiness" interchangeably.

The accepted definition of positive psychology is *"the scientific study of positive human functioning and flourishing on multiple levels that include the biological, personal, relational, institutional, cultural, and global dimensions of life."*

And Martin Seligman went on to explain what he meant by living the "good life" saying he was referring to *"using your signature strengths every day to produce authentic happiness and abundant gratification."*

WHAT CAN WE LEARN ABOUT BOOSTING OUR SELF-ESTEEM FROM POSITIVE PSYCHOLOGY?

The short answer to this question is: everything!

In the definition of positive psychology, its founders talk about the importance of our biology, our background, our personal experiences within our local communities, and our understanding of the global sphere in which we find ourselves. So, this is where we can look for clues about how we can grow and support our self-esteem to find and sustain just the right level. There is another big clue too in Martin Seligman's explanation about what he meant when he talked about "The Good Life.'

He tells us that we need to be using our "signature strengths" every day in order to be authentically happy (not fake happy) and to find meaning in our lives.

This may sound, at this point, just like a whole lot of words. So, let us turn it into a felt experience; let's take some time to discover our own signature strengths because using these will become your secret weapon to leveling up your self-esteem.

As soon as you are able, and with the definition of positive psychology still fresh in your mind, make a list. You can think of signature, in this context, as meaning those qualities and characteristics that represent Real You and that others would recognize as being a core part of who you are and what matters to you.

When you have this list, make sure you save it or keep it somewhere safe. Then, when you have some time, go back to Rick's List which I shared with you in Step 3 (chapter four), where he was talking about the positive experiences the brain can store if we can focus on them, which then allows the mind to change from negative self-talk to a more positive narrative, which will help level up self-esteem.

. . .

Rick's List (again)

- Resilience
- Confidence
- Self-confidence
- Happiness
- Determination
- Compassion
- Self-compassion
- Gratitude

Notice if there is any correlation between any of the core qualities and characteristics you have written down as your Signature Strengths, and if so, give them a big tick. Remember, some words are interchangeable; for example if you wrote "Kindness" then, you can see that as being the same as "Compassion" and give yourself that tick.

I don't know you, of course, but I am willing to wager you have more ticks than you could have imagined giving yourself before you reached this part of the book. And there's a way you will very likely get even more, which is to ask family, friends, and those you feel close to if they could list three of your Signature Strengths that come to mind when they think about you.

Gather all this information, all of which is important in taking Step No. 4 and making it an important part of your own journey toward optimum self-esteem. Keep it in a safe place so you can always go back to it when life gets challenging or when you are feeling over-whelmed. It will connect you, instantly, back to "the good stuff" which, in turn, supports your feelings of resilience, being able to cope, and your feelings of self-worth (self-esteem).

In the final part of Step 4, let's look more closely at some of the traits and adopted behaviors positive psychologists tell us can help live a "good life" and by doing so, foster a more stable and optimum level of self-esteem almost as a by-product of the positive choices we can learn to make.

ACCEPTANCE, OF YOUR PAST AND YOUR REAL SELF

Positive psychologists encourage us to accept our past. It has been and gone, and we can't change anything about it now. Instead of focusing on what happened, what was wrong and whose fault that was, positive psychology takes the view human beings are naturally more often drawn by the future than driven by the past. So, the trick here is to become one of those human beings. We can sum this step up as follows;

- Make your peace with your past and accept it, do not waste any more time placing blame or looking for explanations
- Look ahead to your own future and allow yourself to feel excited and optimistic about it
- Find a feeling of contentment in the present moment and realize that is the foundation of your everyday well-being

FINDING VIRTUE = DOING GOOD, FEELING GOOD

This is such an old fashioned word but it basically means being someone who knows the difference between right and wrong, chooses "right" and has high moral standards that others recognise in you too. Being virtuous does not mean being a Saint at all times but it does mean embracing those positive Signature Strengths that we listed earlier. If you are wondering how this can apply to your everyday life, think about the choices you perhaps already make.

- Perhaps you are vegetarian because you don't like the idea of animal slaughter. You can see this as "a virtuous" lifestyle choice and one which should make you feel good about yourself
- Perhaps you have joined a campaign group trying to half

the destruction of the environment. Again, this can be seen as having virtue

- Or maybe you find your virtuous choices in the spiritual or religious choices you make and the charity work you undertake or donate to

HAVING INFLUENCE

Self-esteem research shows that people who feel they have some influence—those who believe people listen when they speak and have something authentic to say—demonstrate healthier levels of self-esteem. The key word here though is authentic. We are not talking about the Instagram "influencers" who can sell out a summer dress or handbag just by featuring on their stories page. That's a job and has its place but I am talking about the other kinds of influencers. People like Rain Dove who is not afraid to tackle gender issues and put their detractors back in their places with compassion and kindness, even when the trolls are hellbent on firing death threats their way. I am not suggesting we all have to take to social media and start firing our own views out into the world; there are lots of less public ways to feel your voice matters. They say "actions speak louder than words" and so here are some ideas to show you what I mean.

- Join the local political party you support and help them campaign when the next election comes around. Influence and activism are two sides of the same coin
- Lead by example. You can influence the thoughts and feelings of others simply by making lifestyle choices that set a good example to others and show you are "Real"
- Use your consumer dollar to influence what and how companies spend their marketing budget. If you are against animal testing for beauty products, only buy cruelty-free

CELEBRATING ACHIEVEMENTS

Finding and celebrating the good stuff—in your life, in your community and in the world—is an important part of leveling up self-esteem. We saw in Chapter Four how the brain just loves to hang on to the bad stuff, and we understand now that is an evolutionary "hangover" from the days when our hunter/gatherer ancestors needed to identify danger fast and run. But we don't live in those fight-or-flight times, and so our challenge is to get the brain to start storing the good stuff. When it comes to the good stuff and positive experiences then anything that feels like an achievement counts. Here are some things that are achievements which you may not have stopped to think about or celebrate

- You finished school and stayed the course, maybe you also passed exams which will open more doors for you
- You are holding down a loving relationship as well as a busy job and your household is a peaceful and (mostly) happy one

COMPETENCE

Thinking about the things you know you are good at will also start to level up your good feelings about yourself which, in turn, will translate into healthier self-esteem. Do not be modest or shy here, if you are the best cook in the family, then give yourself that title and enjoy that sense of accomplishment. It is tempting, in our Western Society, to judge someone's competence solely based on academic exams and degrees but that is to mistake the diverse and broad range of competencies worth celebrating. Try some of these on for size;

- You are financially responsible and good with money = competent

- You can cook and feed yourself and others a healthy diet on a limited budget if you need to = competent
- You know not to dominate the group in class or in social surroundings because it is important to give everyone their turn to speak = socially competent

Before we run through the last of the Signature Strengths and character traits that positive psychology researchers have identified as being excellent sources of positive self-esteem, just take a few seconds to check in with how you are feeling as you read through this section and think about your own list of Signature Strengths.

Which of these two statements holds true for you right at this moment in time:

1. I am feeling good about some of my Signature Strengths, especially those I have never considered before
2. I am liking Real Me; I am liking Real Me more and more!

WORTHINESS

If you are here, almost at the end of chapter five and Step 4 and still thinking you don't deserve the good stuff and have nothing of worth to bring to the table you may have to dart your Attack Dog (remember him/her from Chapter Three) to send them to sleep for a while so you can access your feelings of self-worth which he/she is so busy guarding they've forgotten to let you past the security and into the protected area.

Actually, it doesn't matter that you don't yet believe you are worth it because you are not yet even half-way through the book and so we can hold that thought and come back to it. For now, take not my word but those of the researcher studying positive psychology: you are worthy. We all are. You have forgotten just how worthy you are and by the time you get to the end of the book, you will have been reminded. Until then, think of three nice things someone else has done for you in the last week or so. If you are struggling, think about mundane, everyday things like:

- Someone put my rubbish out for me to catch the truck on time on collection day
- A friend gave me a really lovely top that she thought would look better on me
- I was picked for the sports team I was hoping would pick me

KINDNESS & COMPASSION

You don't need a list from me to prompt you to remember acts of kindness and compassion. Just think about the last nice/good/kind/important thing you did for someone else or on behalf of your community. Then tell yourself, "Well, I can't be all bad, can I?" If it helps to make a list for safekeeping which you can refer back to when your self-esteem feels wobbly, go ahead but I'm guessing it won't be that hard for you to think of all the ways in which you show a kind and compassionate heart most days of your life. Kindness and Compassion are two of the key ingredients in living A GOOD LIFE!

RECOGNIZING RESILIENCE

One of the assumptions that was made before positive psychology came along was that people who suffered from low self-esteem had little to no resilience and that it would not take much to destroy what little self-esteem they had managed to hang on to, leaving them unable to bounce back from life's challenges. This may be true but if you are here and reading this then you are still alive and have already bounced back, probably multiple times. Even if you only ever bounced back once from something you found difficult to handle an undermining of your self-worth and self-confidence then you have already demonstrated self-esteem. Need a few prompts? How about these three:

- You have had your heart broken, picked yourself up, repaired your heart and gone on to explore a new loving relationship.
- You lost your job and your world collapsed. You accepted help to get back on your feet, took whatever job was going and eventually found meaningful work again.
- Someone you cared about a lot died. It left you feeling life is random, cruel, and callous. Two years have passed and you have made a memorial garden to celebrate the life of that person, along with their other friends.

If you have experienced anything that challenged you, your world view, and your self-esteem but you lived to tell the tale (and read this book) then you have already shown you are capable of resilience. You may need and want a little more and we will look at how to achieve that but it is not something outside your life experience to date so trust that and know that when you need it again, it will be there.

Remember this too; we don't grow because of the good stuff. We grow because of the challenges like heartbreak, disappointment, and grief. Then, when we grow, there is so much more of us to throw into and at the good stuff that will become the foundation of our happiness and living that good life.

Here is your formula for finding your self-esteem inside and outside of you:

Acceptance + Virtue + Influence + Achievement + Competence + Worthiness + Kindness + Compassion + Resilience = External Sources of Positive Self-Esteem

In this chapter we learn that we would have to be working from now on with our Real Self (not the Ideal or Dreaded Selves) and that this would call for us to take an honest look at ourselves.

We discovered the secrets of living "a good life" and learned where we could easily find other important sources of self-esteem.

IN THE NEXT SECTION

- In Part II which comes next, we start the serious work of leveling up or dialling down our self-esteem to find the right (optimum) level for us as we embrace Steps 3 to 10 of our 13-Step Program to Optimum Self-Esteem.

PART II

THE SKILLS YOU NEED TO LEVEL UP OR DIAL
DOWN YOUR SELF-ESTEEM

STEP 3

LEVEL UP YOUR CONFIDENCE

In Part I, we dived deep into the theories of self-esteem so we could better understand what it is and why it is so important to us. In this second part of *13 Steps to Optimum Self-Esteem,* we are going to explore more of the practical steps we can take to start to level up or, if needed, dial down our levels of self-esteem in order to enjoy all the benefits of an optimum level. We will then go on and celebrate all those benefits in the final chapters of the book.

We started to understand that self-esteem can fluctuate and that levels are not set in stone, but that there are multiple triggers that can take their toll on you. Your self-esteem may have felt stable and secure last year, but then maybe something happened between now and then and it all feels a lot more fragile.

So, the foundation of this section—learning those skills we need to make sure we can enjoy strong, stable, healthy and non-contingent levels of self-esteem—starts with learning that self-confidence and self-esteem are not at all the same thing.

One way to see how self-confidence and self-esteem differ is to think about a famous performer who can step on stage and act or sing in front of millions but who goes home at night to try to numb the pain of low self-worth by using harmful and addictive behaviors that may even threaten their lives. Here is someone who has learned their craft and honed the skills to step confidently on stage to all that adoration, but this is also clearly someone who does not love or value themselves!

You can better understand the critical difference between the two when you realize that self-esteem is a "value" judgement that you make about your "Real Self" and your integral worth, while self-confidence is all about self-trust. So, our celebrity trusts they can perform (self-confidence) but hates their Real Self. What this tells us is that self-confidence is not a substitute for self-esteem but it can be a part of the steps we can take to achieve optimum self-esteem because feeling more confident can make us feel better about ourselves.

It may even be that you found your way to my book because you are worried about your self-confidence and that in trying to learn more about how to become more confident you stumbled across the idea that the issue may lie in low self-esteem. So, it then makes sense that while they are not the same, you certainly can't fix one, without fixing the other. And you probably don't need me to tell you that the opposite of self-confidence, which is self-doubt, can be really self-defeating.

So, let's look at self-confidence and see how we can nail it!

SELF-CONFIDENCE: USE IT OR LOSE IT

Do you know the real reason most people never reach their full potential? It has nothing to do with brains, or opportunities, or resources and has everything to do with their belief in themselves or, rather, a lack of belief in themselves. In other words, it is your self-confidence that can propel you toward your dreams and help you to realize them.

It is tempting to think confidence is simply an accident of birth or a genetic gift and that those who have it were lucky enough to be born with it but that is just not true. Confidence isn't some fixed attribute —like the color of your eyes or skin—it is something that is the result of what we think and believe.

Here's an example. Say you feel stuck in an unrewarding and dead end job and you would love to do something more meaningful for work. What's stopping you? Is it that those jobs you would enjoy more don't exist (unlikely) or is it really a lack of self-confidence that is stopping you from refreshing your CV and pitching in for the job of your dreams? What do you believe will happen if you try to change jobs? Do you believe you will find the perfect job for you and easily persuade a new employer that you are the perfect fit for that role or have you convinced yourself that there are so many other people who are better qualified that nobody would ever give you a chance?

What we believe shapes how we think about ourselves and directs our actions. If we believe we will fail, either that is what will happen or, more likely, we will talk ourselves out of even trying rather than risking the humiliation of failure.

We've seen in Chapter Four that we can choose to retrain our brains and change our beliefs. Even better, we can do this at any age and any stage of our lives and one of the beliefs we can start to change is our self-confidence which will be expressed as a belief in our ability to succeed!

Psychologists call this "volitional" by which they mean "it is a choice."

You can become more self-confident but you will have to put in the work. Think back to a time you did well in school or at work. Remember how you felt when people heaped lots of praise on you? Your confidence rocketed and probably stayed sky-high for a while or at least until someone then criticized you about something else, or you felt rejected in a relationship, or you felt unheard and unseen by your family and friends.

I am asking you to revisit these feelings because they show you that self-confidence, like self-esteem, can fluctuate and the good news about that is it means we can make deliberate choices that can give us more confidence. Imagine if you go to the gym or workout in any way that your self-confidence is like a hidden muscle that's gone flabby.

What do we say about muscles? Use them or lose them. It's the same for self-confidence!

So let's now look at some of the ways we can start working our self-confidence "muscle" because the more it expands, the more confident we will feel that we can not only manage but also shape the direction of our lives. In other words, we can get in the driving seat and make sure it doesn't feel as if life happens to us and we are always a victim.

There are really two key ways to learn new behaviors;

1. Fake it until you make it
2. Copy others who have already mastered this attribute

FAKE IT UNTIL YOU MAKE IT

This is the art of "pretending" and who hasn't done that at some point in their lives? You may be full of self-doubt and have such low self-confidence that even pretending feels overwhelming but you can start small. Think about ways you can "stretch" yourself and take a peek outside your comfort zone.

It is true that it is easier to build self-confidence than it is to build self-esteem but there is only one way to train your self-confidence muscle and that is to take a risk. So, you may want to look for your courage as you take this important step. If, for example, you are limiting yourself at work, offer to get involved in a more complicated project the next time one comes around.

If things work out, great. You now know you can do more than you thought.

If things fail, you also win because you now know you can survive a failure and (as we have seen in Part I) even befriend and learn from your mistakes!

COPY OTHERS ...

This is a core tenet in hugely popular and successful self-development programs like Neurolinguistic Programming (NLP) where participants learn to see how someone who is very good at something does what they do.

You can easily do the same.

Is there someone in your life who you admire because nothing seems to defeat them and whatever happens to them, their self-confidence shines through?

Get as close to this person as you can. Watch and observe them and their mannerisms.

- Are they standing tall when they enter a room or do they shuffle in apologetically?
- When they speak, how do they get other people to listen?
- Is their self-confidence brash or quiet and steely?

Watch, listen and learn. Go home and practice in front of the mirror. Then, when the next opportunity comes along to take a risk yourself, imagine you are this same person, grab the chance to shine and do your best to step up.

SELF-CONFIDENCE FOR WOMEN

Research shows that girls emerge from adolescence with a poor body image (see Step 7, Loving Your Body), lower expectations about life and much less self-confidence than boys which explains why self-confidence can be a particular issue for girls and women of all ages. So, let's look at some of the specific steps we women need to take to get that self-confidence muscle strong and ready to take anything on. Here are the ways that women, in particular, can challenge the thinking that results in low self-confidence and change the narrative that is holding them back and stopping them from reaching their full potential.

STEPS TO IMPROVE YOUR SELF-CONFIDENCE

- Identify the beliefs that are limiting you
- Challenge those beliefs
- Banish the negative self-talk
- Change the narrative
- Own your achievements
- Contain your failures
- Identify good role models
- Adopt a growth mindset

Identifying the beliefs that are limiting you: Your emotional triggers will help you identify these. What upsets you, especially in the workplace or any other public arena? How much do you compare yourself with others? How often do you only see the outward success of a colleague and forget they, like you, may have their own private struggles that you know nothing about? Other ways we limit ourselves is by downplaying our own achievements and allowing self-doubt to keep us in our comfort zone.

Challenge those beliefs: If you believe you are rubbish and not up to the task at hand, let's see the evidence. The chances are there is none because this is something you tell yourself to avoid taking a risk and challenging yourself to grow. Let's turn this on its head and see if we can find any proof for the opposite statements. You are not rubbish. You are valued.

Banish the negative self-talk: Go back to Part I of the book and practice some of the ways I've given you of silencing your Inner Critic/Attack Dog.

Change the narrative: Revisit chapter four where we learned how we can retrain the brain to record and store our more positive experiences. Remember that the mind shapes our thoughts and what we allow into the mind shapes our brains. Now think about Real Self vs Ideal and Dreaded Self. Who is the more realistic version? We change the narrative by settling on a story that is more reasonable and more likely to reflect the truth than the scary one we have been telling ourselves for so long.

Own your achievements: Women tend to credit either the circumstances or even other people with their successes. Men do not. This is easy to understand because, historically, little girls have been raised to understand it is not feminine to be seen as immodest, boastful, or competitive and that if we do this, other little girls won't be our friends. This speaks (shouts) loudly at the sisterhood. We don't deny our achievements because of what men think but because of how other women may treat us. This needs to change ...

Contain your failures: Wouldn't you know it ... women who refuse to own their achievements are the first to blame themselves when things go wrong, unlike men who will blame external circumstances or simply say the task was too difficult. Men also tend to "contain" failure to a particular instance, whereas women have a habit of interpreting it as a global way of doubting all their abilities and then questioning their self-worth. So when you fail, sit down and analyze what went wrong, but do not let one failure threaten your self-confidence.

. . .

Identify good role models: In a study of how role models can positively influence a woman's self-confidence, Swiss scientists looked at the differences between men and women who were asked to give a videotaped talk in a room where, either, there were no pictures on the wall, or there were pictures of Bill Clinton, Hilary Clinton, and Angela Merkel. The scientists discovered that in the room where there were no images of role models, the male participants spoke for significantly longer than the women taking part in the study. The same happened in the room where there were photos of just Bill Clinton. But in the room where there were female role models, the pictures somehow closed the gender gap and the women matched the men in terms of confidence and public speaking. The researchers concluded female role models can inspire women and inspire confidence when they face a stressful task such as public speaking.

Adopt a "growth" mindset: Stanford University researcher Carol Dweck has come up with the idea of a Mindset Theory which shows that having a "growth" mindset that is open to change and learning is far more closely linked with success than having a "fixed" mindset which stops us taking the risks we need to take to develop more skills and build self-confidence. With a growth mindset you see every opportunity as a chance to learn and grow. With a fixed mindset, you will avoid any situation that might expose your real or perceived limitations.

HOW MASCULINE NORMS IMPACT WOMEN'S CONFIDENCE IN THE WORKPLACE

Women's self-confidence in the workplace tends to decline as they age. They may, for example, start their careers equally as confident as their male counterparts about moving up the career ladder of promotion. But after just two years in the workplace, studies show their aspirations drop to half the level of those of male colleagues and their confidence has fallen even lower than that by comparison to the men who match for age and experience.

Unsurprisingly then, a recent British study showed that 75 percent of working women felt a lack of confidence in the workplace. With those who had taken a career break, often to raise a family, feeling even less confident when they returned than when they left.

The study of 301 women, carried out by researchers at the University of Glasgow on behalf of an organization called My Confidence Matters, found the women suffered from similar confidence issues, regardless of which sector they worked in and reported feeling especially nervous about the following:

- Asking for a pay rise or putting up their prices (43 percent)
- Standing in front of an audience to make a presentation or speech (40 percent)
- Networking (34 percent)
- Feeling intimidated by their boss or other colleagues (27 percent)
- Competing with colleagues (20 percent)
- Chairing a meeting (19 percent)

Geraldine Perriam, honorary research associate at the University of Glasgow, said: "It is not, and should not be, a given that women experience low levels of confidence due to their gender." Masculinist "norms" that are weighted toward specific, established types of orga-

nizational structure and demands on employees have been demonstrated to undermine women's self-confidence.

Almost 60 percent of the women who took part in the study told the
researchers that networking with "like-minded" women would really
boost their confidence.

"One of the important 'take home' messages of the data gathered in
this survey is that the women surveyed are motivated to improve
self-confidence through training and networking," added Geraldine.
"Building a community and skills development are priorities for the
respondents. It is to be hoped that opting into these two pathways
will lead to a more confident and collegial workforce of women in
the future."

IN THE NEXT CHAPTER

- Now we have seen how we can increase our self-confidence,
  in and out of the workplace, I will show you next, in Step
  4, how to raise your inner voice and get heard.

7

STEP 4

RAISE YOUR INNER VOICE

"You are allowed to take up space. Own who you are and what you want for yourself. Stop downplaying the things you care about, the hopes you have."

— BIANCA SPARACINO

YOU DESERVE TO TAKE UP MORE SPACE

This may sound small, but it requires a huge step and leap of faith from you because in order for you to take up the space you deserve, you have to believe yourself worthy of doing that, and you will also have to break the habit of downplaying what you care about and speaking up for what matters to you.

This won't be easy, but Rome wasn't built in a day. Take your time. We will have a look at the things that may be stopping you from owning who you are and what you want so we can work out how to do something about them in order to allow Real You to step forward and drive the direction of your life.

- You struggle to say no, even when saying yes goes against your beliefs
- You are scared if people see Real You and how vulnerable you really are they will think less of you
- You worry about sharing your achievements and talking about your dreams
- You find it easier to share your mistakes and your failures
- You don't like asking for help
- Your communications are littered with apologies and apologetic phrases which only serve to minimize your contribution
- You have yet to realize people value the contribution you can make
- You have yet to realize how much you have to offer

HOW TO CHANGE THIS WRONG THINKING AND NEGATIVE SELF-TALK

As ever, once we can see the obstacles blocking our path to having the confidence and self-esteem to reveal who we really are, we can set about demolishing them, one by one.

Learning to say "No": Why is it hard for you to say no? You are not alone, a lot of women will "go along with" things just to avoid conflict and even when it goes against their core beliefs. But conflict avoidance is not the only reason. We are raised, as little girls, to be nice, polite, and people-pleasing and so we grow up wanting people to think we are kind, caring, generous, and selfless. But here's the thing. One of the biggest indicators of having a strong and stable level of self-esteem is having the ability to say no. If it helps, tell yourself you are not saying no to the person asking, you are saying no to the request itself. Practice. It is important to communicate your boundaries to others. And as you get better at saying no, try saying no without justifying yourself or over-apologizing. Remember, you deserve to take up space. Practicing how to take up that space will get easier too.

Revealing your vulnerabilities: Being vulnerable is choosing not to hide your true feelings and desires. Yes, it sounds scary and yes, you may feel uncomfortable at first but you will discover something amazing once you start to share Real You with the people around you because you will learn that it is vulnerability that helps us to foster and build the strongest connections with others. A shared vulnerability, for example, allows you both to go beyond a place of fear to have a meaningful conversation about your shared experiences. It is a win-win decision because when Real You makes a connection with Real Them you will both feel supported, seen, heard and understood.

Become your own cheerleader: If you're not going to acknowledge and celebrate your achievements and get excited about your future goals and dreams, who is? Openly sharing your successes can help inspire others to aspire to their own goals and talking about learning from your mistakes and failures can help others see we can all grow from the lessons we learn when things go wrong. If this sounds strange, imagine yourself in a cheerleading outfit jumping up and down on the sidelines of a big match where the star player is: YOU.

Befriending your mistakes & failures: We saw in Part I how a mistake can always be seen as an opportunity to learn, grow, and do better next time, and in Step 3, we saw how women have a tendency to "globalize" their mistakes which means, instead of containing them like men do, we tell ourselves well, if I got this wrong, I must be rubbish at everything! Learn how to keep your mistakes and failures in a "container" marked *"opportunities to learn and grow!"*

Learn to ask for help: Why do you think human beings live in communities—tribes and groups? We have been designed to help each other so our species can survive and even though we no longer live in caves with scary predators lurking outside, there is still a "safety in numbers" and our survival still depends on being part of the human race. Asking for help is not a sign of weakness. It is a sign of maturity and strength because it shows that you recognize your limitations at this point.

Stop saying sorry all the time: Are you someone who says "Sorry," and then tries to speak? What on earth are you apologizing for? What have you done? It is not a crime to open your mouth and share an opinion, a thought, or encouragement with others. This is another opportunity to take up space. When you apologize, you normalize for others that you doubt the value of your own words. But look for that role model here: have you honestly asked for more space than they have? You might have to fake it for a while, but the confidence of your words increases when you remove apologetic language. Let your ideas take up your space!

Your value and your contribution: Speaking up and out is each of us can help to make the world a better place for all of us who share it now and for those to come. Whether at work or just hanging with friends, don't hold yourself back any more. Your opinion matters. You are there for a reason. You are living a life and you are working hard on yourself (you must be, or you wouldn't be reading this right now) so that tells me you have an exceptional contribution to make.

HOW TO BE MORE ASSERTIVE

Being assertive means standing up for your personal rights, expressing your thoughts, feelings, and beliefs in direct, honest and appropriate ways. Being assertive is not the same as being aggressive. When we learn to become more assertive, we do so while still maintaining a healthy respect for the thoughts, feelings, and beliefs of others. So, that means being assertive allows and teaches us to also consider the feelings of others. Win-win!

If you are a people-pleaser, then you are probably more comfortable being passive and going along with the wishes of others because your need to be liked outweighs your need to be heard. Nobody likes to not be heard—either at home or at work—so the problem with adopting a passive and always compliant approach, which puts the needs of others before your own, is that it leads to resentment, and if there is one thing that acts as a death knell to relationships, it is simmering resentment which eventually explodes out of the people-pleaser causing untold damage.

Here is an example of a passive response where an assertive one would have avoided conflict:

Your work colleague asks you to help them finish a task in order to meet a deadline and you agree, even though this means you may fail to meet the deadline for your own task. Then, as you divert your time and attention over to helping your colleague look good and avoid the stress of a missed deadline, you can feel the resentment kicking in. Your own stress increases and you will be the one missing an important deadline because of your need to be liked. How is your mood now?

Let's try a more assertive response.

Your work colleague asks you to help them finish a task in order to meet a deadline and you say, explicitly, I would be very happy to help you but I have a deadline I need to meet first. Let me see if I can finish this task a little earlier and then I can help you with yours. Your colleague immediately feels supported and hopeful that you may be able to help; their task now feels less daunting and the looming deadline more manageable. Their stress declines but not by passing it on to you. You really would like to help them if you can, so you have coffee at your desk, instead of heading out to the coffee shack, and that means you finish your task early and have the time to help your colleague. Win-win. Nobody is stressed or full of resentment.

BEING PASSIVE AGGRESSIVE

People who find it hard to stop being passive will often respond to a request in a passive-aggressive way which is always a give away that resentment is bubbling not far from the surface. Say, for example, you ask your partner to clean out the fridge. They don't want to do it but they don't want to say no so they say something like, "Sure, I'll do it after I've put the shopping away, made the dinner, washed the baby, filled in the tax return ..." The list goes on. But what are they really saying? They are saying how can you even think about adding another job to my already long to-do list which I am already feeling pretty pissed about. And make no mistake, you'll have heard that loud and clear. Passive aggressive responses are designed to make the person in the firing line feel badly enough about a request so they won't ask again. It is an effective tactic but an unpleasant and unnecessary one.

What would have been a more assertive response to the request to clean out the fridge?

How about, "I am sorry. I would like to help, but I have quite a long list of jobs to get through and I don't want to say I will do it and then not do it because I ran out of time."

Would that more assertive response make the person asking feel so badly they won't ask again? No. They would understand there are other jobs on the priority list today.

BEING AGGRESSIVE

There are so many ways in which being aggressive is nothing like being assertive, but if you're not sure whether you'd be able to tell the difference, take a look at these:

- An aggressive response does not consider your feelings or needs
- An aggressive response will not give you time to consider your own response so you may feel rushed into a decision
- An aggressive response will "tell" rather than ask
- An aggressive response is one where you are simply ignored, so "ghosting" on social media, for example, is aggressive
- An aggressive response is designed to make sure you do not respond assertively
- Manipulation is a covert form of aggression
- Humour can be used aggressively, think about a time you were the butt of someone's unkind joke which others laughed at

It is important you learn to distinguish between these three behaviors and types of responses: aggressive, passive or assertive. The better you can "read" the room and a real life situation, the better you can respond assertively but appropriately so that your own needs are not trampled.

Good communication, as ever, is key!

HOW TO COMMUNICATE BETTER

We have seen how being assertive can help us improve our communication skills by making sure we make it clear our own needs are important. In this step where we are learning to "raise" our inner (and outer) voice that starts and ends every sentence with an apology can be a sign of low self-esteem.

There are other words we might like to think about dropping from our vocabulary in order to improve our communication skills and develop an ability to mean what we say and say what we mean. These include words such as;

Actually—don't be the know'all in the room who has to correct everyone, all the time

But—using this word just makes sure everyone forgets what you just said or dismisses it as unimportant

Dude—unless you want to deliberately sound immature leave this one outside the door of the college classroom

Fault—nobody is really interested in the "blame game." People pay more positive attention to solutions-focused communications

Honestly—If you have to say this at the start of a sentence it implies you were not being all that honest before

Just—Ban, ban, ban, ban, ban it! I am just a homemaker. I was just asking ... This is a small and usually unnecessary word with the potential to do a lot of damage in translation

Personally—"Personally, I think ..." If it is your thought then it can only be personal to you and you don't need to say so. Just say, "I think ..."

Unfair—You are right. It is. Life is. But nobody wants to hear this coming out of an adult's mouth. It will make you sound like a whiny child and everyone will stop listening the instant you say it.

WHEN YOU BECOME ASSERTIVE ALL YOUR RELATIONSHIPS WILL IMPROVE

Being assertive means being direct and honest with people. You don't expect people to read your mind about what you want, and if something is bothering you, you speak up and say so. You don't beat around the bush and if you need something you ask for it.

You do all this in a calm and civil way which respects the rights of others.

When you are assertive you understand that while you can ask for something or share an opinion, others have the right to say no or disagree with you and you don't get angry or upset if that happens. You stay in control and you work together to reach a compromise.

When you are assertive—when you have learned to raise your inner voice—you understand you might not get what you want but you also know not asking makes it less likely to happen so ask anyway.

You can think of assertiveness as being the golden mid-point between passive and aggressive behaviors and once you learn to ask, assertively, for what you want and need, you will find both your self-confidence and your self-esteem rise to new and (importantly) sustainable levels.

SHYNESS VS. SOCIAL PHOBIA/SOCIAL ANXIETY

It may be that you struggle in any social or work situation because you are shy and always have been, or there may be something stronger going on like social phobia, also known as social anxiety. Again, these two are not the same thing, and here is the key difference: shyness is a personality trait. When you are shy, you don't like the limelight or being at the centre of a conversation but a social situation does not trigger anxiety or distress.

When you suffer from social phobia (social anxiety) you can experience high levels of distress as a result of any social situation and may have learned to avoid social gatherings altogether. Social anxiety often emerges in the teens or young adulthood and you will know you suffer from it if any of the following cause serious distress:

- Talking in front of other people
- Going to parties
- Talking to strangers
- Eating, drinking, writing or using your phone in front of other people
- Using public toilets
- Using public transport
- Waiting in a line of people

If you do suffer from social phobia (anxiety) then you will likely already have experienced some of the following symptoms that can be triggered by your distress:

- Nausea
- Hand tremors
- Excessive perspiration
- Quickening heart rate
- Blushing
- Difficulty speaking and only being able to speak in a quiet voice
- Feeling self-conscious
- Feeling embarrassed
- Feeling everyone is judging you negatively

Experiencing any, some or all of these symptoms can be enough to trigger avoidant behavior and leave you finding ways of avoiding social situations but happily, there is an effective treatment which means you don't have to stay home and avoid society for the rest of your life.

Social anxiety has been shown to be very effectively treated using a technique called cognitive behavioral therapy (CBT) which involves changing your thinking and the way you then approach these potentially triggering situations.

CBT will help you to identify negative thinking and self-talk and challenge it, but you will need to find a qualified therapist who uses this technique to learn it. In a 2016 study by Norwegian and English researchers, CBT was found to be effective in treating social anxiety. Some 85 percent of those sufferers taking part in the study said they noticed significant improvement, however, the same study also identified that only a third of those coping with social phobia will come forward for treatment which means this is a condition that often remains hidden.

Sufferers don't like talking about their anxiety and, understandably, cannot face the prospect of a doctor's waiting room where there will be other people i.e., another social setting. If you recognize yourself in any of these signs or symptoms then you can take this online anxiety test to confirm or allay your concerns: https://www.nhsinform.scot/illnesses-and-conditions/mental-health/mental-health-self-help-guides/social-anxiety-self-help-guide

IN THE NEXT CHAPTER

- In the next step, **Step 5**, we will learn how to face more of the fears that can be blocking the way to achieving a stable and optimum level of self-esteem.

8

STEP 5

FACE YOUR FEARS

Did you know that your brain thinks it is doing you a favor by using the powerful mechanism of fear in as many guises as it can think of to stop you from reaching your full potential and to hold you back? Just like the brain's negativity bias, which we explored in Chapter Four when we examined ways to retrain the brain, hanging on to fear is an evolutionary throwback. It is true; there was a time way back in the lives of our ancestors when it was fear that kept them safe and as a result of that ability to discern when to run and hide, they stayed alive!

Today, we don't face those kinds of real-life deadly threats from predators or other external circumstances, but our brains don't know that. They are simply doing the job that they have been designed to do. And, if that means keeping you in your comfort zone and stopping you from taking on new challenges and risking failure, then so be it.

If your brain can't find and react to one real enemy—like a prowling grizzly bear or some other real life threat—it will unleash its protective mechanisms into your everyday life bringing fear into otherwise harmless scenarios where it really has no place to be.

Fear has been put in place to keep you (safely) in your place, but the real enemy is not what happens to us but what we fear may happen. Fear can be so powerful it feels paralyzing, and fear can be so sneaky and subtle, you've barely noticed it creeping in and curtailing your freedom and choices. But we can't grow if we don't face our fears at some point and by facing them, we come to understand that, luckily, for most of us, fear today is something we can learn to manage and even overcome.

Remember how we learned to disarm the Inner Critic or "Attack Dog" in Chapter Three? Well, we will need to employ the same sneaky techniques to disarm fear because it's not going to just walk out of the door you are holding open as you try and give it its marching orders. So, what we are going to do instead, in this Step 5 of our program toward optimum levels of self-esteem, is to recognize fear when we feel it, thank it for being so protective, but tell it we've got this and can handle whatever perceived threat on our own.

The only way to disarm fear is to take charge of fear and your reactions to it. And while we are at it, we may as well take the same stance with those tricky emotions that often roll in alongside fear when it is unleashed. I am talking about those feelings that are rooted in fear; things like anxiety, doubt, imposter syndrome, and judgement—especially judging yourself harshly.

The way to disarm all these negative thoughts and feelings is to do what the yogis, buddhists, and others who use meditation practices for well-being do—acknowledge the thoughts as they come into your head but send them on their way because they are not needed.

If the idea of regulating your thinking this way is new to you, and if you are not sure how to start getting back in control of those feelings which can otherwise leave you feeling frozen in fear and self-doubt, just take a tip from those with more experience. If it is too much to swap a negative thought for a positive one, then just use a simple phrase or word which you can repeat silently in your head until the negative stuff has passed. You can even come up with your own affirmation which you repeat every time fear, and its friends, come along.

You might try saying something like:

I am healthy. I am whole. I am connected. I am loved, just the way I am.

Choose words that mean something to you but make a commitment to using the exact same words or phrases each time Fear and its cronies are about to strike. You will already know the tell-tale signs; your hands might start sweating and you may feel your heart beating faster. You feel a sense of panic rising up to your throat and feel the urge to run away. Instead, stand your ground because most of the time, your fear is imaginary—and repeat the words you have chosen either aloud or inside your head.

In some esoteric practices, this is known as Mantra—the repetition of sacred words or phrases to banish unwanted thoughts and fears.

You will likely feel a bit odd when you first try it and perhaps even struggle to believe it can work, but the more you practise it, the more natural it will feel and before long, it will be your automatic response when you can hear and feel fear and its unwelcome companions knocking on the door of your mind.

Disarming your fear, just like disarming your Inner Critic, is proven to work. But it may take time and patience. It can also help if you are able to discern a little more about why fear has shown up again, and to do this, we will now take a look at some of the key fears that can not only stop us in our tracks, but block any kind of forward movement toward a brighter future.

Let's start with the biggest one of these—Fear of Rejection.

FEAR OF REJECTION

We are taking this major fear seriously and here's why. When scientists decided to look at the portion of the brain that is activated when people are asked to remember a painful rejection during an MRI scan, they discovered something absolutely astonishing: the part of the brain that experiences, records, processes, and stores the experience of an emotional rejection—the same part of the brain that experiences actual physical pain.

So, it is true. Rejection is painful and just as painful as any physical wound.

Now let's look at what happens when we are reeling from the pain of this kind of rejection. Yup, here they are; the Inner Critic (or Attack Dog) and Fear. It is as if this painful rejection has opened the doors in your mind to a free for all and these two are at the front of the line to get in.

If your heart has been broken and you are devastated by feelings of rejection, you may be angry and bitter that this has happened to you. The science supports that you are experiencing actual physical pain, but the rest is all down to you because the deep and lasting pain of rejection is the pain you inflict on yourself and your self-esteem.

"Oh, I know," says Inner Critic, "Let's play the blame game. Who shall we blame for this latest catastrophe which feels like our world has ended?"

"Well," says Fear. "There's only one person that springs to mind and that's you-know-who."

Guess who Fear is pointing at? Your Inner Critic is nodding and together they are about to put out the bunting because once again, not only have you demonstrated how absolutely useless you are when left to your own devices, you've also opened that closed door, let these two back in, and shown how much you need their protection.

"Now look," says Inner Critic, adopting a soft, nurturing tone as they wipe away your tears. "We all make mistakes, it's just that yours are always worse than anyone else's. But don't worry because my good friend Fear is here, and so together we can make sure this never happens to you again. Ok?"

"That's right," says Fear, puffing out his/her/their chest with pride. "You're safe with us. We won't allow this to happen again. We won't allow anything to happen!"

And so the stage—a lonely one if you listen to these two and allow them to rule the roost—is set for the next chapter where the moment someone shows any kind of interest in you and your feelings, you are gone. Pouffe. Like a little magic trick. All disappeared in a puff of white smoke, never to be seen (around them, at least) again.

Inner Critic and Fear can't resist an all-night party. You've toed the line, you've allowed both of them to run your life and as far as they are concerned, they're doing such a good job keeping you away from life—and the risk of any more rejection—they should both be up for a promotion.

But while Fear and Inner Critic crack open the canned cocktails, you are quietly sobbing in the corner of the room. It's true, you tell yourself, you are safe and cosy in your lonely comfort zone. But there's another voice that's just a whisper at the back of your mind and this voice is saying something else...

This voice is saying, "No, put your foot down and don't let Fear and Inner Critic run and ruin your life. You may have just missed out on someone special because you let them scare you into compliance."

What this tiny little voice wants to shout is: "Get up out of that corner, take back your power, and get back out there again. Rejection is horrid but it won't kill you, however painful it feels at the time."

3 STRATEGIES FOR DEALING WITH REJECTION

Perhaps that tiny voice is not enough to get you back out into the world but maybe these three tried and tested strategies will give you the courage to risk everything—including rejection—again.

Strategy (1) Have Zero Tolerance for your Inner Critic (Attack Dog)

Strategy (2) Do something that boosts your feelings of self-esteem and self-worth

Strategy (3) Reach out to strengthen your social connections

Zero Tolerance for Your Inner Critic (Attack Dog)

We've just seen how your Inner Critic has been off celebrating the fact you are now afraid of any further rejection with their old friend Fear but the person who has allowed this is you. The good news about this is that this means you are also the person who can get them back in their respective stations and tethered back up again and the way you do this is really, really easy.

You tell them—and by doing so, you are also telling yourself—this one simple truth that nobody can argue with, not them and not even you.

The fact is most rejections, whether romantic, professional, or social, are due to circumstances that have NOTHING TO DO WITH YOU.

That's right. You simply can't take credit for something that was going to happen despite you, regardless of you, and in no way because of you. Maybe your new beau or girlfriend just wasn't ready to commit to anyone or maybe the place that turned down your job application found an internal candidate who was a better match for the role. You just don't know.

The only way to keep from blaming yourself is to banish Inner Critic and Fear with a new Mantra or, if you prefer, Affirmation and with this one, you can leave nobody in any doubt who is in charge of your emotional life and your levels of self-esteem.

This is what you need to tell yourself and keep telling yourself until you believe it. It is perfectly acceptable to fake this attitude until you make it:

"I see rejection as an opportunity to learn and grow, rather than any failure on my part."

The Things That Make You Feel Good About Yourself

Remember your lists of Signature Strengths from Step 4, and how I suggested you keep that list somewhere safe so you can go back to it? Now, when you are feeling the pain of rejection, is the time to do that. Read the list out loud. Every night, before you go to sleep and every morning when you wake up. Memorize it so you can repeat it to yourself whenever you need to bolster your self-esteem.

Now remind yourself of these things: You Are Important. You Are Loved. You Matter To People.

Get Out and Meet People

Human beings are social creatures and hiding away licking your wounds after a rejection can serve to compound the feelings of hurt. You may end up feeling hurt by the rejection itself but also isolated and lonely because you've chosen to hide your shame.

Forget that. You Are Important. You Are Loved. You Matter To People. So, get in touch with someone who will remind you of that, someone you may not have seen for a while because you were so engrossed in your relationship. Someone who will be really pleased to hear from you. Get in touch and get out of the house.

Yes, you may still be in pain and yes, you may want to come straight home again so you can cry some more but this is tough love right here. Nobody ever got over a rejection or heartache by sitting feeling sorry for themselves, night after night. Eventually you have to dust yourself off and get back out into the world where you will discover something wonderful—the world has been waiting to tell you how pleased it is to see you again for the whole time you have been in hiding!

SOCIAL REJECTION

There have never been more ways to reject each other; ignoring a WhatsApp message, swiping left on Tinder, failing to like an Instagram story, ghosting someone after a date or two, both online and in real life.

No wonder it can seem to Millenials and those born afterwards, that the world is just one big social "ouch!" or that lots of people, after multiple rejections, decide a night in with Netflix is less risky than another Zoom date.

I am not saying this stuff doesn't feel personal and isn't hurtful; it does and it is but the only person you can turn this into a learning curve is you and that is a decision you need to actively make and pursue.

One of the key things you can do when it comes to building better resilience against these seemingly casual social rejections, is to stop assuming the worst and give someone the benefit of the doubt. If you are honest with yourself, you may be feeling hurt over someone you barely knew, and so actually, you really don't know what may be going on in their lives or the real reason they ghosted you.

I'm not saying make excuses. I am saying the other person is simply irrelevant here. What matters is what you tell yourself, so stop telling yourself you are rubbish/nobody wants you/this was all your fault, or any of the other unfounded Inner Critic bilge you could spout all night—except I'm not going to let you.

Learn to detach a little. These social rejections are not a matter of life or death, and in a (very short) while, you probably won't even remember the name of the person who has hurt your feelings right now.

Ask yourself this: does it really matter? Do you really care or are you making a drama out of something that wouldn't even get your attention if you were out there having fun with your family ,friends, and the people who know and love you?

And each time you feel yourself slipping into the self-blame game just remind yourself of your Signature Strengths and of everything Real You brings to the table.

FACING CRITICISM

Ask if the person who likes criticism will put up their hand and reveal themselves and don't be surprised with a no show of hands. None of us will get through life without being on the end of criticism and none of us like it. The smart thing to do is to prepare some strategies for the next time something uncomplimentary comes your way. This will not only train your brain to better handle criticism, but by doing so, it will better protect your self-esteem.

There are only three types of criticism; so your first task is to decide which category the offending statement(s) fall into and then act accordingly. These three categories are:

- Irrelevant
- Destructive
- Constructive

Dealing with **irrelevant criticism** is easy: don't. You can ignore it and decide not to dignify it with a response of any kind from you. Of course you will feel annoyed but let it go ... stay detached and if you absolutely have to have any feelings on the subject, feel sorry for the person who has nothing better to do with their time and energy than make some pointless and irrelevant remark that won't win them any friends. This kind of behavior is their problem, not yours.

Destructive criticism can be difficult to handle because it is always so unkind (and usually untrue too). So, again, you are going to focus on the person choosing to behave this way, rather than what they say or why they say it. When it comes to making mean statements and observations about another human being, what is said is more of a reflection of the meanness of the person saying it than it is of the being being criticized this way. Do not engage. Walk away. Remember, if at all possible to steer clear of this person moving forward.

Constructive criticism is the mature way to deal with the only kind of criticism worth paying any attention to. See it as an opportunity for learning and improvement. You will begin to notice that someone, say a boss, who is very skilled at constructive criticism, will deliver the "learning lesson" in the middle of a "sandwich" where the outside layers acknowledge how well you are doing and when things have gone right.

We then dip into the "filling" which might be a comment calling to your attention the fact that by rushing a task you forgot to include key elements—the take home message here would then be perhaps slow down—and then we come back to the second outside layer with another compliment about your willingness to listen and learn.

It is a fantastically effective way of delivering constructive criticism, and you will know when you have been the recipient of constructive criticism because you will walk away from the exchange feeling good about yourself and your willingness to learn and improve.

Here are some really good tips for dealing with criticism when it shows up without losing your cool or making matters worse.

1. Never respond to any type of criticism in anger. This only takes the focus off the person who is being critical and onto you and will make you look bad, even when the criticism has been unfair and unjustified.
2. Listen carefully to what is being said and remain cool, calm, and collected throughout
3. You can challenge destructive criticism by saying something like, Why would you say that? What evidence do you have? But, if it looks as if the situation is likely to become

overheated, walk away. Standing up for yourself is a good sign of good self-esteem. You do not have to be doormat for people to thoughtlessly trample.

4. Unless the criticism is irrelevant, in which case you can ignore it, treat the other person with respect and understanding. This shows maturity and that you are a Class Act.

5. If you have made a mistake which is now being pointed out, put your hand up, own it and say you will learn from it and take care not to make the same mistake again. Everyone appreciates honesty.

FEAR OF FAILURE

Fear of failure has its own name—atychiphobia which really just tells us it must be very common. It's true that we will all run into feeling scared of failing at one time or another in our lives and will avoid those situations where we feel we might end up feeling shame or embarrassment because we fail to live up to what was expected of us.

What might make you feel scared of failure will not be the same as what scares another person so only you know the outer limits of your comfort zone and the ways in which fear can or does hold you back when you edge up to those limits.

- Have you ever said no to something you secretly wanted to try but felt too scared to risk because you might fail?
- Are you reluctant to try new things or take on challenging projects in case you fail?
- Has being rejected made you fearful of dating or getting close to someone else again?
- Did you not get called back to the second round of interviews for a job you had thought you were "a perfect fit for," leaving you feeling scared to knock on any new doors?

If any of the above apply to you then you are letting your fear of failure hold you back. If you want to change this habit which will only get worse if you ignore it, then start by trying to work out what failure means to you?

Do you think Michael Jordan, one of the greatest basketball players of all time, allowed fear of failure to bring his potential to a sudden halt after he was cut from his school basketball team? Or did he pick himself up and risk yet more rejection to follow his dreams and find a way to showcase his extraordinary talent to the sporting world?

Warren Buffet is one of the world's richest and most successful investors and businessmen. You might want to ask how come Harvard University failed to spot his potential and turned him down when he applied to study there?

The world is full of examples of people who overcame their own fear of failure and, even more impressively, of failing again to chase their dreams and reach their full potential. Your own family and friend-ship groups will have people who have had to pick themselves up after major disappointment and risk it all again.

It is not easy risking it all and there are good reasons why some people, especially those suffering from low or fragile self-esteem, may struggle more than most to overcome this fear. Fear of failure can also be traced back to childhood experiences, including having critical or unsupportive parents which generated negative feelings that have survived into adulthood.

That said, in some studies of early school learning, fear of failure was identified as an issue for the children of hot-housing parents who delivered too much praise, all of the time and who had high and unrealistic expectations of their child doing well in every school test, all of the time. These children, even the brightest among them, soon learned to avoid doing more challenging tasks in case they failed so in this case, fear of failure set in for entirely different reasons.

Fear of failure can also be based on a bad experience or a traumatic event. If, for example, you were asked to speak in public but failed to prepare properly and then made a mess of your presentation, you may have left that experience feeling so wounded and scarred by embarrassment and shame you could never contemplate putting yourself through such a trauma again. It may also be that initial trauma and fear of failing again has now tipped over into other areas of your life.

HANDLING MISTAKES

Self sabotage is a big clue that someone is suffering from fear of failure and unsure of how they should respond if they do make a mistake in public. These are the people who you may meet who seem to procrastinate and never really get started or get finished— which is a surefire way of avoiding failure at all costs!

But the thing these people—and you, if you are amongst them—are really missing out on is the opportunity to fail and through that failure grow in character, grit, resilience and knowledge. Talk to anyone over the age of 50 and they will tell you all the biggest lessons of their life came from failure and learning how to handle mistakes. And if you think about it this makes sense because if you take something on and execute it perfectly, what is there for you to learn and how would you grow? You already know how to do it, there is no learning there for you.

A lot of successful entrepreneurs will look back at their long careers and give thanks for those early failures that taught them to sharpen their skills, go back to school to study or change direction in the career of their choice. What all these people know is something I will share with you now: failure will not destroy you, unless you let it.

Here are three fantastic lessons that failure has to teach us. These are the kinds of lessons you can only really learn from experience and they represent the hard-won knowledge we may see in people older than ourselves and refer to them as: wisdom.

THE THREE BIG LIFE LESSONS FAILURE HAS TO OFFER

- Failure is what will help you face your fears head on
- Failure will teach you what works and what doesn't
- Failure will show you who your tribe is; these are the true friends and mentors who stick with you through the good times and the bad. There may not be as many of them as those who were hanging around when things were going well but each of these tribe members is worth a dozen of those others

When you see the benefits of failure shared in a list like this, it makes you want to rush out and embrace all the experiences which may trip you up and leave you with a little egg on your face because as we've now seen, you've really got nothing to fear and everything to gain from every experience of failure that comes your way over your lifetime.

MOVING ON WHEN YOU'VE MESSED UP

You have something else up your sleeve that will help you to recover from any failure or mistakes you may make and to do with good humour and good grace and that secret power of recovery is your sense of humour.

Nobody likes the idea of looking like an idiot in public but nobody ever died from that either. You are allowed to wallow—for precisely one day—and then you need to try and see the funny side.

Humour is a powerful healing tonic and not least because it allows us to keep perspective when we feel things have gone wrong, our self-esteem has taken a nosedive and everyone is laughing at us and our mistakes.

One thing you need to tell yourself is "hey, you're really not that important". We live in a world where "Selfie" has become a noun and honestly, most people are way more interested in themselves and their own dramas to get involved in yours.

If you need to apologize to anyone about what has happened do that, do it sincerely and get it out of the way and then move on. If anyone else wants to keep raising it, raise an eyebrow (you can practice this in the mirror at home before you have to face them all again) and then make it clear you have moved on.

We are not defined by our mistakes or our failures. We are defined, if we need to feel defined, by our Signature Strengths and those qualities that make us the Real Us.

Take your lesson from your mistake and take the view that actions speak much louder than words. Prove your worth and your value by making sure you did learn a valuable lesson and one you won't need to repeat to learn again. Notch it up—or down—to experience and remember that when it comes to learning about life and reaching our full potential, no experience is ever a wasted one.

In Step 5 we have learned to name and face our worst fears and see how they may be holding us back from reaching our full potential and living our best lives.

We learned that the biggest teacher in life is failure so to fear and avoid failure is to fear and avoid growing as a human being, and we have also learned some excellent strategies for handling mistakes, learning from them and making sure we don't have to repeat them

IN THE NEXT CHAPTER

- In the next chapter, **Step 6**, you will learn how to be kind to yourself.

STEP 6

BE KIND TO YOURSELF

Have you ever heard someone throw out the line, "Well, she clearly loves herself" as a criticism of the way someone has just behaved? Have you ever heard anyone say, "I see she loves herself" as any kind of compliment? For some extraordinary reason, we are raised—especially women—to think that loving ourselves and taking loving care of "us" is just selfish and wrong.

How many people do you know who are really kind, caring, and considerate of others and then really mean and unkind toward themselves? If you were to bring Real You into this conversation right now what would they say? Would they say, "Hey, you've just described me!"

Loving and caring for yourself is a skill and one many of us never learn because we feel too guilty to put our own name at the top of the Needs My Care List. This is downright daft because if we don't look after and love ourselves, we won't have enough care and compassion to endlessly give to and care for others. We will run out and then feel angry that other people didn't notice we were running out of steam because we were always running about looking after them!

If you think about the safety instructions the crew give us whenever we board an aeroplane, it's not all the stuff about the lifejackets, whistles, and inflatable exit slides that is memorable, it is the part where you are told to take care of yourself first by putting your own oxygen mask on before you try and help anyone else.

Let's unpack that a little before we submerge ourselves in a chapter that is all about showing you why your name needs to be at the top of your Loving Self-Care List.

If something goes badly wrong and your oxygen mask drops from the ceiling mid-flight and you don't put it on before trying to help others, what do you become? You become one of those who needs assistance. It really is as simple as that.

The trouble is, persuading anyone with low or fragile self-esteem they are worth the time and trouble of self-care care and self-love is a herculean task because there are so many obstacles they will already have in place blocking the path, including guilt and, worse, worrying that putting themselves first in any way will make them seem narcissistic.

So for those of you who may be tempted to skip this important step because the idea of being kinder and more caring toward yourself feels just plain wrong, stay with me, and I will show you why it is so important on so many different levels, including the one where we are shining the spotlight on how you feel about yourself and how this, ultimately, translates into your all-important self-esteem.

LOVING YOURSELF IS NOT THE SAME AS BEING A NARCISSIST

When you understand and can show yourself love, nobody is going to start calling you a narcissist because the word "love" means something very different to those who deserve that title. With a healthy self-love, you don't need to put someone else down in order to bring yourself up and so you don't need to spend your time comparing yourself to others in order to fake self-worth and self-love.

With healthy self-love, you can (and should) take pride in your performance and achievements, and you can give yourself the praise you deserve for these, but you are also able to accept there are times when you are full of doubt and not sure how to behave, react, or respond.

With a narcissistic self-love, all that really matters is how they "look" to others. They have not done the inner work of becoming the real deal (Real You) because they are too busy craving validation from others and pretending to be something they are not.

Narcissistic self-love is dishonest and focused on other people; healthy self-love is honest and self-focused.

Healthy self-love, then, is an honest and authentic appreciation of the self; narcissistic self-love is all about proving you're better than everyone else and making sure others know it, which is very sad because really this is just a mask to hide their buried feelings of no self-esteem and no self-worth. As we have seen, if they had either they would not so desperately need the validation of others.

GUILT-FREE SELF LOVE AND CARE

Learning to love yourself is just that—a learning experience and the people you will be learning this from are the people who are already in your life and who show they love and care for you. This will likely be the same people that you asked to help you write your list of Signature Strengths, so before you do anything else, make a note of all their names which we will return to shortly.

Psychotherapist and author of a book called *Deeper Dating*, Ken Page, writes about learning self love in an article in *Psychology Today*, where he explains that it is impossible to will or think our way to self-love; it is a feeling we have to learn from others. He says: "As much as we want to control our own destiny, the humbling truth is that sometimes the only way to learn self-love is by *being* loved—precisely in the places where we feel most unsure and most tender. When that happens, we feel freedom and relief and permission to love in a deeper way."

"No amount of positive self-talk can replicate this experience. It is a gift of intimacy, not of willpower. In my work as a psychotherapist, I've found that we tend to be ashamed of our most unique, passionate, and iconoclastic parts. These aspects of ourselves threaten our safety, but as I explain in my book, they are the direct path to love, and, not incidentally, to personal greatness. When we suppress these challenging gifts, we're left with a sense of emptiness and loneliness."

It is astonishing to think that the shame we feel around our most vulnerable attributes is a shame that is universal and because of this, not even our best thinking, says Ken, will budge it. So, how do we escape from the clutches of this learned shame that is stopping us from being our Real Selves and expressing all our gifts?

The best and sometimes only way out is through our relationships but only those relationships which reflect back to us the deep worth and value of our most vulnerable self.

This, then, is your proven path to an authentic self-love based in an authentic self-care.

SURROUND YOURSELF WITH THE PEOPLE THAT BRING OUT THE BEST IN YOU

It sounds like the obvious thing to do, doesn't it? But be honest, is it what you do and have done through your life? Have you selected for friendship—and love—based on knowing this is someone who is rooting for you, who gets you, who likes you, who champions your gifts and talents, and who genuinely wants you to do well and achieve your goals?

Or do you have people in your life who quite like to keep you in your place which is, essentially, somewhere below them. These would be the people who feel threatened by your talents and gifts. They would never admit to it but they are jealous of you and the bed-fellow of jealousy is usually ... spite!

You will know when someone is being spiteful because you will feel it. You probably won't understand it or their motives for being mean but your gut will tell you to protect yourself by putting some serious distance between you and their little spiteful comments and observations. Of course, you won't because the truth is, you can't quite believe anyone would feel they have to be jealous of you—or mean to you—because you can't see quite what you have that they could possibly be jealous about. (If you need a reminder, go back to Rick's List and your Signature Strengths from the previous chapters).

This is why we need those people who do see what it is about you that might make less secure people, and those with more fragile self-esteem want to belittle or shame you. They could give you a long list of what's so great about you that it can make (some) others want to spit or at least keep you down and "in your place."

RELATIONSHIPS OF "INSPIRATION"

In his book, *Dating Deeper*, Ken Page says these are the relationships which not only see but also relish Real You. These are the people who are not afraid of your passions and they are not jealous of your gifts. They have the generosity of spirit to want you to grow and reach your full potential without having to hide or compromise who you really are, and these are the people who have no doubt that you are worthy of love, friendship, and respect.

Take a few moments to think through the people you have in your life right now and pick out the names of those who meet the criteria above.

These are your Relationships of Inspiration.

These people, says Ken, are "gold" and the ones you want to hold on to. He suggests "practising" surrounding yourself with people like this in your social life and friendship group so you can really experience being Real You, so that when love comes along in a romantic sense, it will be Real You that you take into that relationship too.

LACK OF SELF-LOVE EXPLAINS A HISTORY OF TOXIC RELATIONSHIPS

If you have a sorry history of failed romantic relationships and are still struggling to understand why, think back to the quality of those unions, and see whether any of those ticked the boxes to qualify as a Relationship of Inspiration or whether someone (you) was faking a lot of the time because you were too scared to show Real You. If you are going to admit to that then you've just worked out—without the expense of a good therapist—why that relationship, and probably others too, was never going to last.

Those relationships were not based on true and lasting love. They were based on a false notion of how you both thought you should be; perhaps you were both trying to bring Ideal Self to the union and to keep Dreaded Self out in the cold. Sadly, what you succeeded in doing was leaving Real You on the doorstep too.

Hopefully, you are now beginning to see what self-love and self-care is so important in forming lasting relationships and loving unions and not least because subliminally, we tell people how we want to be treated. If you can't be bothered to take better care of yourself or it is obvious when you meet someone new you have zero love for yourself then you are pretty much giving people carte blanche to treat you badly from the get-go.

If, on the other hand, you show up as someone who has taken the time to look carefully and see (for yourself) the wonderful qualities that your "Relationships of Inspiration" reflect back at you then it is clear from the get-go to everyone who meets you that you are someone who expects and deserves love and kindness, and respect, and that is what you will get.

And if not, it is plain for all to see that you—and your self-respect—will be up and out the door ...

MAKING SELF-CARE A PRIORITY

Now we have seen why self-love and self-care is so important in shaping all our relationships, and the way we treat ourselves sends very clear signals to others about our hidden feelings of self-worth (or lack of), we can unpack what gets in the way of self-love and self-care because by understanding the obstacles, we can think about how best to remove them and allow guilt-free self-love to flow in our lives.

Here are some of the main reasons you have not learned the art of self-love and self-care and once we have examined these, we will turn this on its head and look at the things you can do to take better care of yourself and show the world that you have self-love.

- We think self-care is the same as being selfish; it is not
- We flip into "rescue" mode to save others as a way of avoiding taking care of ourselves
- We give too much so our relationships are based on neediness, not sustainable love
- When we give too much and don't practice self-care and self-love we run out of resources, burn out and feel resentment which is the death knell to any relationship, romantic or platonic
- We teach people it is ok to take, take, take from us because we don't have enough self-esteem to say "*Stop, that's enough!*"
- We expect others to take care of and be responsible for us, rather than learning to do this ourselves

- We think other people are worth more than us and until this attitude changes, we will continue to attract people who agree with this misconception

If we go through the list above, we can see some clues about how to go about learning and then practicing self-love and self-care. The first of these clues requires us to understand and believe that self-care is not the same as being selfish. Go back to the start of this chapter and re-read what I said about the on-board safety instructions when you fly. Who do you have to take care of before you try and save anyone else? You now know the answer, so whenever there is a choice —your welfare or someone else's, try and make the choice that is based on self-care. Then, when you are in good shape and have a surplus of love/time/energy/money or whatever you can offer by way of support to someone else, you can do so. But remember, the key word here is support. Supporting someone who may be struggling is not the same as rescuing them. It is not your job to recuse anyone. It is not healthy to rescue others as a way of avoiding taking care of yourself!

Lots of people who struggle with issues that stem from having low or fragile self-esteem are the nicest people you will ever meet. They have learned, somewhere along the way, to ditch their own authentic and perfectly acceptable needs (= no self-care) to put others first, and if there was an Oscar for being a people pleaser, these are the people who would win, hands-down. Are you one of these folk? Are you the one who puts everyone else's needs before your own and so, of course, everyone says they love you. They don't. They like the convenience of Ideal You who is so busy helping everyone else, Real You is drowning.

Do you know the poem, "Not Waving But Drowning" by the British poet, Stevie Smith? She published this poem in 1957 and in it, she describes a man who has gone swimming in the sea and found himself in trouble. He is signalling to the people on the shore who can see him but who think he is just waving. He is not. He is in serious trouble and drowning. And from the opening lines of the poem it is clear he is dead.

It is a chilling and haunting image; that of someone who needs help but whom everyone thinks is doing fine. Is this you sometimes? Do you ever feel that people just assume you are cheerily waving when, in fact, you are drowning because you have depleted all your resources and have nothing left to give to the takers? It is a sad fact that people will take until you say, "Stop, that's enough." So that's on you—if your signals are being misunderstood then either change them or spell them out for people. And when you say "enough" make sure you damn well mean it!

TIPS FOR PRACTISING SELF-CARE

The single most important thing you can do when you start to think about practising self-love and self-care is to invite Real You into the room to do the work, and leave Ideal You and Dreaded You outside the door, where they belong anyway!

Set aside some time before you move on to Step 7 and the next chapter to acquaint yourself with how your particular brand of self-love will look. Make yourself a favorite drink—coffee, herbal tea, whatever you think of as a treat, and start with a list of the things you know you could do (and probably don't) that are a demonstration of serious and authentic self-care and self-love. If you are struggling to get started, here are some prompts;

1. Eat three healthy and nutritious meals a day
2. Learn or practice some relaxation techniques, such as meditation or yoga
3. Find a way to connect with yourself in a meaningful way; this could be through one of the well-trodden esoteric paths such as yoga or shamanism or martial arts. Find something that goes deeper than sport for its own sake
4. Get some outdoors exercise every day

5. Try and spend time in Nature, which has been shown to be essential for our mental health and well-being and so is an important part of self-care and self-love. If you live near a forest you could take up the ancient Japanese art of *shinrin-yoku*, which is a contemplative practice also known as Forest Bathing.

6. Take a break from your social media and stop worrying what other people think about you. What's important is what YOU think about REAL YOU

7. Whenever there is a choice about which version of you shows up, try to choose REAL YOU

8. Spend time taking nurturing of your "Relationships of Inspiration" and make sure you protect this circle of friends

9. Weed out the so-called friends who are jealous of your gifts

10. Try and find ways to have more fun and to take yourself and live a little less seriously from time-to-time

PRACTISING SELF-CARE AND SELF-LOVE WHEN YOU ARE IN A COMMITTED RELATIONSHIP

Sometimes, despite all the good work we have done on ourselves, self-love and self-care fly out of the window the moment we make a commitment to another person, and by doing so, default back to our people pleasing ways to make sure they will continue to love us. We've already seen how a lack of self-care and self-love can lead to resentment or worse, a toxic relationship that continues to feed our lack of self-esteem and self-respect, so it is worth taking some time to think about how you can maintain self-love and self-care when romantic love comes knocking on your door.

SELF-CARE IN A RELATIONSHIP

- Take time to be alone
- Set boundaries
- Manage your stress levels

It is hard to find the time to check in with yourself when you become entangled with the life of someone else, but it is crucial you find the time to do this because the healthier you are, the healthier your relationship can be. The truth is you can't be a good partner if you are struggling with your own self-worth, and we've already seen how time out to take care of yourself works to support your self-esteem.

Boundaries in a relationship are crucial too. You should talk to your partner (and keep talking) so that you can manage your expectations about how the relationship will work and support you both, as well as making sure you are on the same page with the practicalities. For example, if you are out with friends for the night, will your partner expect you to let them know what time you will be home? If your partner is out will you be stalking their social media to see who they are hanging with? These may sound like small issues but they can easily blow up into big ones. When you are not on the same page with boundaries, someone who keeps overstepping boundaries will be someone you will find very hard to live with in a harmonious and supportive home.

When we are stressed—because of work or some other event—we may feel we are heading toward becoming Dreaded Self and set up a cycle of feeling stressed about that too! Nobody is at their best when dealing with high levels of stress so try and stop yours from escalating or at least take up some relaxation techniques so you can dial down when you know you are at risk of flaring up.

SELF-LOVE IN A RELATIONSHIP

- Stay present
- Recognize and accept the importance of your feelings
- Find meaning, and even a spiritual connection, in your life which will support you through the ups and downs that every relationship will encounter

People talk about the painful experience of online ghosting on dating apps or new dates that simply disappear off the radar with no explanation when everything seemed to be going so well, but nobody talks much about the temptation to "ghost" your partner when you are in a committed relationship because you feel as if your feelings will overwhelm you.

Ghosting within the relationship is what happens when you switch off instead of doing the work and sorting out boundaries on how you can both maintain self-care and self-love. Ghosting is what happens when you decide you're not investing in this relationship any more in the same way and go on the missing list, but don't bother to tell your partner. You will be in the same room but it will feel, to your partner, that you are not present at all and that's because you have checked out emotionally. Don't let this happen because it is hard to claw back from. Trust Real You if an issue needs resolving between you and discuss it, instead of "ghosting" each other.

What feels spiritual to one person will leave the next feeling cold, but it is important to find meaning in our lives and only you will know what "speaks" to you. It could be a traditional religion or a so-called New Age practice. You don't have to share this with your partner, and you shouldn't expect them to find meaning in the same way too, but it is important to develop this resource for yourself because it will help support you in your relationships and carry you through both the good times and the bad. Finding meaning in our lives is also a fast-track route to finding our lost self-esteem or building one that has been fragile and in danger of crumbling at the first external challenge. You may not yet know what will bring meaning to your life, but that doesn't matter because you will enjoy the journey you can take Real You on to find that answer!

In Step 6 of our 13-Step Program to Optimum Self-Esteem we have seen how important self-love and self-care are when it comes to building stable and sustainable self-esteem

- We've learned self-love and self-care are not the same as narcissism or selfish behaviors
- We have also explored the multiple ways in which we can put ourselves first and take better care of our own needs, before concerning ourselves with the needs of others

IN THE NEXT CHAPTER

- In **Step 7**, I will share with you the importance of learning to love your own body regardless of skin color, race, size, and age.

STEP 7

LOVE YOUR BODY

LOOK IN THE MIRROR (FULL LENGTH). WHAT DO YOU SEE?

Y ou will probably need to be brave because you are going to take all your clothes off and take a proper look at your physical body—head to toe! Make sure you have complete privacy and won't be interrupted. Shut the door, and use a hand mirror so you can take a good look at your back view and everything you don't normally get to see, as well as the front. Before you get undressed and start, take a moment to usher Ideal You and Dreaded You out of the door and close it firmly behind them.

Once you are naked, go and stand in front of the mirror and take a good, long and honest look at your body. Don't skip over the bits you would rather not see (and would much rather nobody else saw either!) You know the bits I mean ... we all have them because nobody is perfect and that's why we sent Ideal You out of the room. Equally, nobody is so far from perfection that what they will see reflected back in the mirror will be so bad they feel ashamed to step out of the front door or stride along the beach in swimwear. Your body, just like Real You, will be a mash of things you like, things you'd like to change and things you'd rather hide.

As you take the time to really look at your physical self, and to look, using the hand mirror, from as many different angles as you can pay attention to the Self-Talk. What judgements are you hearing? Is the Self-Talk you are hearing negative or positive? What is the tone of the voice being used like? Is it kind, or is it harsh and critical?

Once you are finished really looking properly at your body, you can put on a robe or get dressed again so you are warm and comfortable because I want you to think about and answer the following question with as much honesty as you can:

"How do you honestly <u>feel</u> about your body and what you have just seen?"

If you are not sure about what to say or where to start with this honest appraisal of your physical self, here are some prompts:

When I look at my body, I feel ... happy/unhappy

When I look at my body, I feel ... proud/ashamed

When I look at my body, I feel ... love/hate/nothing

And here are some more triggering questions you can ask yourself so that you can better experience all the feelings you have about your naked body:

The part of my body I like best is ...

The part of my body I dislike most is ...

The part of my body I try hardest to hide with my clothes is ...

Now ask yourself a final question about all the answers you have given which is this question: Why?

WHAT MAKES YOU FEEL BAD ABOUT YOUR APPEARANCE?

The first step in learning to love our body is being honest enough to look at them and see what we don't like but the really important step is understanding why we judge this body—which is actually a walking, talking biological miracle—so harshly.

Did you wake up this morning after a good night's sleep, either waking to an alarm or the sunlight streaming into the room? If so, who took care of that? Who made sure you rested and woke at the correct time? Your Body.

Did you enjoy a delicious meal with friends at the weekend? If so, who took care of all the invisible processes that need to happen for you to digest your food and eliminate any waste? Your Body.

Did you perform well at work and feel a sense of pride in that achievement? If so, who made that happen? Your Brain, an integral part of your physical body!

We could fill the whole chapter with a long list of all the miraculous ways your body takes care of you, does what you ask of it and keeps on doing all that (unless we fall sick) and what thanks do we give it? None. Or worse, we complain about it and wish we could change it so that we walked about in a body that perfectly matched some perfectly irrational social media version of the ideal physique.

Unfortunately, we cannot separate body image from our self-esteem. And if you have ever been present when a slim and attractive person declares they need to lose weight then you already know this because your Inner Critic will have jumped in and pointed out you are at least a stone heavier so if anyone needs to lose the chub, it's you, not her!

There is a reason stick-thin bony models say stupid things like: "*Nothing tastes as good as being thin feels,*" and why so many Western women have a secret code that we all, silently acknowledge, which is that: "*the thinnest person in the room always wins.*'

Wins what?

Some kind of unhealthy competition that underpins the narrative running in our heads ever since we were little girls telling us that we are not [**fill the blank for yourself ...**] enough, good enough, thin enough, pretty enough ... The list is always endless!

I have a friend who happened to live next door to an A list film star who started dating a Victoria Secrets model. My friend was horrified one day to see this tall, skeletal vision in white wafting her way down the path to knock on the front door and pick up a package that she was care-taking for the couple who had been out when it was delivered.

The model, who was beautiful and used to gliding down the catwalk, had a warm smile and held out a bony hand to introduce herself before taking the package. My friend was shocked by just how cold and thin her fingers were. "I wanted to scoop her up, wrap her in a blanket and offer her a cup of homemade soup," she says. While the model was stunning and seemed to be a kind-hearted soul, standards that the industry needed her to meet pushed her to sacrifice health for aesthetics.

BODY IMAGE AND SELF-ESTEEM

How you truly feel about your physical body has been shaped by cultural and social factors, as well as historical ideals about what constitutes "beauty." And one of the key influencers about who will have shaped how you now (even as an adult) feel about your body was someone who may still be having a say in how you look and how you could be "improved" to fit some idealistic mold—that person is your mother.

If you think back to the first time you became aware of your body and how others saw it, what do you remember feeling and why? Did you climb a tree and feel empowered that you had a body strong and agile enough to shimmy up the trunk, or did you try on a dress at the Mall and scan your mom's face or that of the adult who had taken you shopping as they silently handed you the larger size?

Sadly, the loudest voices throughout your childhood and adolescence will have been the voices of those who lived in the closest proximity to you: parents, siblings, best friends, and classmates at school. And somewhere along the line, you understood what was being said to mean something much more than the words themselves conveyed because when someone said "not for you, this would look better" what you heard in your head was:

"I am too fat/big/ugly and not worthy of love and admiration."

Followed swiftly by:

"If I can become less fat/big/ugly then I will be worthy of love."

And there we have it. Almost in an instant and almost invariably overnight, a careless comment, an observation that was meant well but heard wrong, and what lies ahead is a lifetime of low or poor self-esteem!

According to an article published in the American Medical Association's *Journal of Ethics,* there is now an abundance of medical literature telling us what most girls and young women already know, which is that suffering from a poor body image is common and can even start in children under the age of ten.

For example, in an Australian survey of 24,055 young people aged 15 to 19 years, researchers reported that 87.9 percent of the adolescent girls who took part were concerned about their bodies. This same survey found body image ranked third of the top three personal concerns for both genders (coping with stress was No. 1 and problems at school No. 2 on the list) which is a trend academics have noted as being consistent since 2013.

One trend the literature reports is that over time, more girls consider themselves to be "too fat" with slightly more older girls (45.5 percent) starting to diet than younger girls (40.9 percent). The study also found that girls increasingly diet and restrict food intake as they grow older.

Body image and dissatisfaction over the way you look is a serious health issue and is linked with higher levels of depression, impaired emotional well-being, low self-esteem, less health promoting physical activities and more eating disorders.

But how did we get here? How has this happened?

DYING TO LOOK GOOD?

Historically, if you are born a woman in a patriarchal society, then your body has been your best survival tool. Your size and physical characteristics would have been required to "fit" into an ideal determined by male desire and whether a man would want to marry you.

This means your body, your appearance, and your health will have been heavily influenced by the social and cultural ideologies, beliefs, and values of the day, which you would have been expected (and will have wanted) to conform to. Now, if you are not shouting "but what's changed?" at me, then I can only ask, why not? Because we both know the answer: nothing.

Nothing has changed.

Historically, women have made decisions to try to transform their bodies into an idealized shape and comply with these cultural dictates. In Victorian times, that meant wearing a movement-restricting corset and crinoline hoop to achieve the comely house-glass shape that was so admired at that time. It will sound so disempowering to us now but the closer you could come to achieving the "desirable" shape, the more potential suitors you could attract and with that choice, you found your power in being able to choose the wealthiest and the best provider.

In 1843, using corsets to restrict a woman's waist to just 18 inches became so culturally and socially powerful that the Parisian Fashion magazine, Les Modes Parisiennes, declared a woman had to wear a corset in order to be considered beautiful, thus further condemning women of all ages and classes to the considerable health hazards of tight lacing. These included fainting (due to restricted lung capacity), heart palpitations and in some serious cases, muscle atrophy and spinal deformities. And in 1890, the British medical journal, *The Lancet*, ran an article called, "*Death from Tight Lacing.*"

In other cultures, a woman's body equated to her beauty and her beauty equated to power too. In Ancient China and the Tang Dynasty, for example, a woman was expected to have a tiny "willow waist," and you will have read or heard about the foot bindings used to cripple the feet and keep them tiny and doll-like too.

Today, the poor body image a woman can suffer from because she does not conform to the "idealized" bodies she is bombarded by in magazines and on social media, is just as damaging as it was to the long line of our female ancestors. Poor body image is sinister because it cuts much deeper than simply feeling unhappy about the way you look. In our society, the physical body has become the social body to be looked at—and appreciated or judged negatively. Your physical body, therefore, dictates whether you are considered beautiful and thus links to our perceptions of power, health, wealth, and overall success.

With health, wealth, and success comes the ability to make choices, something that can support your feeling of self-esteem. Without these choices, a woman may struggle for years to feel good about herself, whatever her Signature Strengths and capabilities.

It is wrong but it is true that Western societies favor the beautiful which is something little girls learn young, and unless they fall into that revered group, are in danger of living with the consequences of feeling and being excluded for a lifetime.

No wonder then, it is so hard to look in the mirror and like what we see. It is not just tempting to blame all our failures on how we look —it is what women have always done!

THIS BODY TYRANNY CROSSES RACIAL BOUNDARIES TOO

In academic studies that explored the link between racism, self-esteem and shame, challenges discussed by participants included those associated with depictions of African American hair as less attractive and less professional-looking. So, while African American, Asian and Hispanic women all score higher than white women when the researchers measure self-esteem as a result of body image perceptions, their self-esteem can decline as a result of racism or perceived racism.

This demonstrates the key point that it is life experience, more than genetics or personality, that shapes your levels of self-esteem over your lifetime and so not surprisingly, those who are subject to racial slurs and stigmas will struggle to keep the self-esteem, as they do feel that has its basis in a sense of ethnic pride and racial socialization.

The trick, then, is to keep a sense of that pride and the boost to your self-worth from being a loved and loving member of a family and/or local community and to try and not allow racism when it rears its ugly head to derail that sense of self-worth.

GEN Z AND SELF-IMAGE

If you are a member of the generation born after 2000 (Gen Z), then you are the generation of women that has had the hardest time of all trying to hang on to any sense of positive self-image. You have had a lifetime being bombarded by idealized images of the perfect body since early childhood and certainly since you unwrapped your very first mobile phone.

There are four types of self image, and you don't need a degree in psychology to see the enormous impact living with and under the spotlight of social media your entire life will have had on all four types;

THE FOUR TYPES OF SELF-IMAGE

1. Self-image resulting from how an individual sees oneself.
2. Self-image resulting from how others see the individual.
3. Self-image resulting from how the individual perceives others see them.
4. Self-image resulting from how the individual perceives the individual sees oneself.

There is no question that social media has a negative impact on self-esteem. This is because when we use social media, we cannot help but make what researchers call "upwards" comparisons between ourselves and others.

And when we do this, the outcome tends to be that we see "others" as being better than us—prettier, thinner, more photogenic, and having an overall better life experience, all of which combine to lower our levels of self-esteem.

We can make both upward and downward social comparisons, but on social media we tend to make more upward ones, where we perceive and believe someone else to be performing or doing better than we are in important ways.

In one study, designed to test this hypothesis, 150 business students were surveyed by researchers who found that 88 percent made social comparisons when using social media and of that 88 percent, 98 percent of the comparisons were upward social comparisons.

The research also revealed the strong relationship between social media and self-esteem, where an increase in social media usage results in a decrease in levels of self-esteem. For example, just one hour spent on Facebook everyday results in a 5.574 percent decrease in the self-esteem score of that individual.

It is quite likely you spend more than an hour a day on social media because researchers have also discovered those addicted to social media platforms are most likely to be female, young and single. An addiction to social media has also been linked with higher levels of narcissism (which we have already seen has nothing to do with higher levels of healthy self-esteem) but lower levels.

In one Scandinavian study, researchers found that posting about feelings and venting on social media predicted low mood, low self-esteem, and high levels of paranoia. The same held true when the user perceived themselves as being of low social status. However, posting about daily activities predicted increases in positivity and self-esteem or simply viewing newsfeeds reduced these negative outcomes.

Nobody is telling you to stop posting or to delete your social media accounts, but just being more aware of the likely impact on your mood and feelings about your own self-worth if you are spending hours each day telling yourself everyone else has a better life than you (upwards comparisons) is definitely not good for your self-esteem.

MAKE FRIENDS WITH YOUR BODY—IT'S WITH YOU FOR LIFE!

In her book, *Body Wars*, the author Margo Maine teaches us how to reclaim and even begin to love our bodies for everything they give us and do for us.

Here are some of the ideas she suggests that will help you stop criticising and start making friends with your body. You might, as you work your way through the list, want to write down some of the affirmations and post them somewhere you can see them everyday, and you might want to pay special attention to suggestions No. 3 which would remove all body dysmorphia and body image misery if we all decided to wise up and see ourselves this way!

1. Tell yourself your body is perfect the way it is. Make this a daily affirmation!
2. Think of your body as a tool. Make a list of all the fantastic things you can (and do) do with it.
3. Walk with your head high. Feel pride in Real You and get your confidence from knowing you are a person, not a dress size.
4. Make a list of all the people you admire and say why. Now circle all those whose success and accomplishments were due to the way they looked.
5. Do not allow your body image or the fact you think you are big, stop you from doing anything you might enjoy.

6. Ditch the self-criticism and use that time instead to do something fun and healthy.
7. Wake up in the morning and turn the light switch on—the one that allows your individuality and your inner beauty to shine like a beacon.
8. Think back to a time you liked and enjoyed your body as it was. Connect again to those happy feelings.
9. Befriend your body and be its ally, not its enemy.
10. True beauty shines from the inside out and is a reflection of Real You. Love and enjoy the person you are and the person you are on your way to becoming.

Remember:

- Body tyranny has ruled the lives of girls and women for generations but you have the power to stop it now and set an example to all the other females in your life.
- Walk down the street with your head held high remembering you are a person, not a dress size.
- Limit how much time you spend on social media and when you find yourself making upwards comparisons i.e., comparing yourself unfavorably to others, stop and do something more productive with your time.

IN THE NEXT CHAPTER

- In **Step 8**, you will learn how to connect to your Inner Peace to help build optimum levels of self-esteem.

11

STEP 8

CONNECT TO YOUR INNER PEACE

I f you were to stop and think about your life and the way you are living it right now, would you say you are happy or even content with how everything is working out for you? Or do you feel that life is something that engulfs you, sending you spinning in all kinds of directions without even asking your permission, let alone giving you a choice about which direction that might be.

Every life will face challenges, large and small, which means every person needs to develop the inner resources—tools, if you will—that they can draw on to keep going when the tough times hit. And for all of us, one of the most powerful of these inner resources is a sense of inner peace that is available to us all, if only we can find it.

Now, nobody is born like a baby Buddha, chanting their way from cradle to grave with such perfect non-attachment that nothing ever throws them off or derails them. Inner peace does not come as an automatic birthright—although the potential to find and harness it does so that is what we will focus on in this chapter.

The world can sometimes feel like a mad and uncaring place, especially when external events and circumstances throw things at us that are destabilizing and likely to take a toll on our self-esteem. I am thinking about things like the "triggers" we explored in the early chapters of this book, including the "biggies" like job loss, divorce, relationship breakdowns, pregnancy loss, and living in poverty.

You are not born knowing how to navigate and cope with these kinds of challenges, your job is to learn from others and from your own experience to grow the resilience you need to cope, without losing your own sense of humanity and what really matters.

Inner Peace is one of the building blocks of resilience and in this chapter I will define exactly what it is and show you how to find and connect to your share of it.

If Life (with a capital "L") has its say, you won't have the time to work with Inner Peace so right at the outset, you need to make a commitment to treat this as a priority. It will be a commitment that you won't regret once the tough times hit.

People sometimes think Inner Peace is all about adopting some spiritual dogma and practice, and it is true that some belief systems, including Buddhism and say a daily yoga practice, will put a special emphasis on connecting to and working with Inner Peace, but this is not the exclusive territory of any of those practices.

We can learn a lot by observing what works for others and so we can choose to adopt some of these "spiritual" or more "religious-sounding" techniques but we do not have to sign up for that tradition itself. We are, crucially, free to choose, even in the face of difficult life events.

In some ways it might be easier to understand precisely what I mean when I talk about Inner Peace by understanding better precisely what it is not.

INNER PEACE IS NOT ...

- Being passive and allowing life to just pass you by
- Being calm all the time and never having any fun
- Turning down opportunities to grow by trying out new things
- Having no physical energy because you are keeping it all contained inside yourself
- Being a quiet, reserved, or even timid person

INNER PEACE IS ...

- Achieving happiness and content not through the things we acquire or anything we achieve but simply by reconnecting to yourself (Real You)
- Becoming a fuller version of yourself (Real You) not by adding in new layers but by rediscovering what has been there all along to support you
- Being whoever you want to be but being an even better version of that person because you have the clarity and presence of a calm inner self
- Letting go of superficial worries and stresses that are weighing down your mind (aka don't sweat the small stuff)
- Accepting everything—your life, your career, your body,

your everything—so you can authentically change and
change for the better when you are ready and choose to

We understand that change can be challenging and difficult but we
have also seen, in the Steps that have gone before this one, that the
best way to implement the changes we want for ourselves is to
understand what is still blocking our way. Once we know what these
are, we can go about removing them so we can, in this case, find our
Inner Peace.

Here is a list of beliefs that really don't serve you when it comes to
reconnecting to Inner Peace; and worse than that, they may be
blocking your path to Inner Peace. The good news about that,
though, is that if any of these resonate you have now identified them
and can now confidently set about removing them to clear the way
to Inner Peace.

BELIEFS THAT BLOCK YOUR CONNECTION TO INNER PEACE

1. I will be happy/happier when I get this: You already know this is false. Think of something material you yearned and even worked hard for. Did it do the trick? Think back to a time when you thought a new relationship was all that you needed. Did that happen and take away your self-doubt or buried anger about the way your life has been going so far?

2. Showing my true feelings will make me look weak: False. If you are not showing your true feelings then you are not being Real You and we've already seen in earlier chapters that nothing is really sustainable until this is the version of you that you allow to take charge and guide your life and your decisions.

3. I must never get angry: Why not? What are you afraid will happen if you show your displeasure? You may be shocked to hear this but anger may just hold the key to the door that you need to open to find your Inner Peace and lead your most productive and meaningful life. (I'll explain how and why later in this chapter.)

4. I need to be doing something right now: Says who? You are a Human BEING. So, try just being from time-to-time. This letting go of the need to be busy and doing all the time is a fast-track way to find greater Inner Peace.

5. I'm not good enough: Good enough for what or for whom? And what's really going on when you tell yourself this, over and over again. Well, your self-esteem is taking a "drubbing" for starters, but maybe you are making excuses so you can avoid the work required to change. Telling yourself this is like giving up before you've even started. Of course, that way, you can never fail but equally, you can never gain either!

6. I am ashamed of my past: Welcome to the closet which is full of old skeletons. We all have them hidden away and we all worry about them coming to light. But we cannot move forward to reconnect with Inner Peace if we are holding on to a bunch of self-recriminations, harsh judgements, grudges, and regrets. Open the closet door and let them out. You will find them a lot less frightening in the light than lurking behind a closed door in the dark. We all make mistakes—it is called growing up and learning, and you cannot find your way to Inner Peace unless you accept every part of your own story.

We can see by this list that finding our way to Inner Peace is a process that is going to require some work from us and the bulk of that work is the work of LETTING GO.

Stop with the self-recriminations. Ditch the victim mentality and try to strike a balance between being accountable for things you now wish you had never done and taking on the blame for everything— including those external events that were outside your control.

One of the biggest steps toward cultivating Inner Peace, is knowing the difference between that which you can control (e.g., your own reactions, thoughts, and values) and that which you cannot. I think you will find one of the big anti addiction programs teaches this as an integral part of learning to heal and if you pay close enough attention, life will teach you it too!

MANY ROADS, ONE OUTCOME ... INNER PEACE

There are so many roads to finding Inner Peace we could fill another book with just half of them but there are, to my mind, two that you can take, especially when you are starting out, that will pay dividends each and every day. They teach you how to make space (in your mind and your busy life) for Inner Peace and how, once you connect to it, to stay connected.

Here are my two favorite roads to Inner Peace

1. Simple meditation.
2. Simple practice of non-attachment.

SIMPLE MEDITATION

Science has now proved what people who meditate will tell you: regular peaceful practice of meditation calms the mind by changing the brainwaves to the more calming theta pattern that signifies the switch from a busy brain to one that is alert and aware but calm too.

Some people want to run a mile when they hear the word meditation but that's just because they don't know that it does not have to be complicated. You do not have to sit cross-legged. You do not have to chant "*om*" or burn incense. Of course, if you choose to do any of these things, all power to you, but they are not a prerequisite.

Find a short meditation practice online and make a commitment to practice for just one week and then review whether you have a better understanding of Inner Peace at the end of that week. Remember, you won't get the benefits unless you actually do the meditation.

But remember too, simply becoming absorbed or lost in a favorite hobby or pastime, such as painting, music, or taking care of your houseplants, can trigger the same feelings of calm, well-being, and Inner Peace. The choice is yours but do something because Inner Peace does not know you are calling and will not, without some effort on your part, just show up at your door.

Some people use the terms meditation and mindfulness interchangeably and it is true that once you practice meditation you do become more mindful or more aware of yourself and how you are. People who practice mindfulness, especially through meditation, have often reported that it's relaxing and reduces stress. Mindful people understand their own emotions and that of other people better and so are better able to react to stressful events better and handle issues more calmly. Mindfulness research has also shown how it can lower the incidence of Social Anxiety Disorder (SAD)

SIMPLE NON-ATTACHMENT

Non-attachment teaches us to be more in the present and to allow the past to stay in the past, as well as allowing the future to unfold. You can think of this shift in thinking as being almost like becoming an "observer" in your own life. Imagine you are watching how one scene leads to another to tell a story—your story—but that you are not the lead actor or even the director; you are someone who is sitting in the audience paying close attention to what happens and why.

Non-attachment does not mean you do not care what happens. Of course you will care, but you won't allow your expectations to dominate your thinking and leave you disappointed every time something turns out a different way from how you expected it to be.

One of life's biggest lessons is that Life (capital "L") is what happens when you're busy making other plans; and once you have enough life experience tucked under your belt, you will see how one event led to another and one (unexpected) outcome can turn out to be the best thing that ever happened to you.

The first thing you can practice havin a non-attachment to is Ideal You. And then try having a non-attachment to Dreaded You. See how you can still be aware these imaginary versions of you exist but how by letting go of being attached to them, they lose their power.

That is the trick with non-attachment. It is a simple but clever technique that restores power to its rightful place which is with you and your well-being. You can also think of non-attachment as being the Art of Relinquishing Unnecessary Control which in turn becomes the Art of Banishing Unnecessary Stress & Drama from your life.

SOLITUDE

This is a word that often alarms people—especially those who cannot tolerate for a single second the idea of being "alone." But solitude is not about being alone, it is about spending time with someone you know very, very well—yourself!

Think of something you enjoy doing but have never considered doing by yourself. This could be visiting a museum, taking a trip, or eating out in a new place that's just opened in your town. Do what you need to do to plan this experience, and do it with the person who should be your best friend and your biggest support—you!

Now, you may feel strange and even a little self-conscious, especially if you decide to eat alone. But you will, if you remain open and don't cheat with this task, discover there is something very calming and very peaceful about spending time with yourself. Without the distraction of conversation or everyday chat with a partner, you will find yourself becoming more aware of not only everything around you but how you fit in.

If you travel alone, you will find others will gravitate toward you and want to know more about you. They would never do this if you are travelling in a pack or as one of a duo. If you eat alone, you will find you may pay more attention to what is on your plate and how it tastes in your mouth. It is a completely different experience and one that you can only have if you choose, from time to time, to eat alone.

Alone is not the same as lonely. Alone is a state which, just like Inner Peace, you will need to cultivate in order to feel comfortable with solitude but it is well worth the efforts you will go to because by embracing solitude, you can also embrace a new connection with Inner Peace.

CONNECTION

In the same way that solitude (above) can help foster a connection to your inner resources of Inner Peace, connecting with and spending time with one of your Relationships of Inspiration (see chapter four) can do the same thing, especially when you both decide to spend a day together doing something that is just fun and light-hearted. Maybe choose something from your Self-Care list and do that together or try something new that you've both wanted to try.

Feeling connected to the good in your life will help you to connect to the Real You and Real You can open the door to Inner Peace because Real You can recognize it and its worth in your life.

CONTRIBUTION

Have you ever heard of something called the Helper's High? This describes the incredible surge of feelings of contentment and good-will that follow when you choose to do something kind or good or helpful for someone else with no thought of reward or payment. Volunteer for a charity and you will see what I mean. There is no feeling like it and guess what? You can't buy it or bottle it or bury it when it wafts like a warm wave of well-being over you after you have given your time, energy, talent, and purpose to something or someone else for free.

Making a contribution to something other than your own life and progress is another fast-track route to finding and maintaining your Inner Peace. When you focus on helping others your own petty concerns will melt away and you will simply feel calm, peaceful, and happy, but don't take my word for it—try it for yourself!

FINDING INNER PEACE BY BEING IN NATURE

Being outside in Nature—and even just looking at images of Nature —has been shown to reduce feelings of anger, fear, and stress and to confer greater feelings of peace and well-being. In fact, Nature has now been shown to be so important to feeling positively about ourselves and our lives that when we are denied it, scientists use a term called Nature Deficit Disorder.

We all need exposure to nature and when we can get outside, whether to walk, exercise, grow things (flowers or food), or even just to watch animals in their natural environment, we feel calmer and more connected to our own Inner Peace. Here are some of the ways that being in Nature can help:

- Your mood improves
- You feel less stressed and angry
- You feel more relaxed
- You feel healthier
- You are more confident
- Your self-esteem is good
- You benefit from getting outdoors and being more active
- You may meet new like-minded people and widen your connections

- You may find more peer support amongst these new connections

Whichever path you choose to help you to recognize and reconnect with your Inner Peace, make sure you pay attention to how differently you begin to feel once you start this process. Notice the impact on your self-confidence and self-esteem because as these improve, you will feel even more motivated to find the time to do the things that connect you and keep you calm.

This is what's known as a Virtuous Circle and, as we have now seen, is one that will work to help you build up to an optimum level of Self-Esteem.

REMEMBER

- We all have an inner Resource that we can connect to in order to build a stable and optimum level of Self-Esteem, this resource is our Inner Peace
- You don't have to meditate or chant to find Inner Peace and the clarity of mind it brings with it, you can simply absorb yourself in a favorite hobby or pastime and connect that way
- Nature wants you to be and feel well and so being out in Nature is another fast-track way to finding your Inner Peace

IN THE NEXT CHAPTER

- In **Step 9**, you will learn how to Master Your Emotions to help you to build optimum levels of self-esteem.

STEP 9

MASTER YOUR EMOTIONS

Mastering your emotions is an important step in building an optimum level of self-esteem, because until you do, you will feel you are at the mercy of feelings that can feel overwhelming and which you may struggle to control. But before we can master our emotions, we need to connect to them and we do that through our feelings.

Think about some strong emotions you may have experienced over the last few months and then think about how these emotions felt in your body.

- Were you sad? Did your body feel light or heavy?
- Were you anxious? Did your body feel relaxed or jittery?
- Were you angry? Did your head feel fit to explode?
- Did you want to cry? Was there a painful lump in your throat?

Once you start to locate the physical experience/sensation of a strong emotion in your body, then you can begin to work on that to regulate and diffuse them, and by doing so, reclaim your power and self-esteem. But first, you must accept and not fight them.

Accepting our emotions can be hard because sometimes we feel guilty about having them and almost always we would rather not have them. They are uncomfortable to experience and we can often feel worse before we feel better. But fighting powerful feelings is not the answer because then they just intensify. You will know this if you have ever tried hard not to cry when you feel overwhelmed by sadness or you have tried even harder not to laugh when something has hit your funny bone.

Accepting our emotions is the second step in mastering them and the only way to diffuse some of the power they have over us. For instance, in one study which looked at how sufferers dealt with chronic pain, those who decided to accept their discomfort and who used mindfulness techniques to cope with the pain reported a 40 percent reduction in the intensity of that pain over time. Accepting any difficult and painful feeling, physical or emotional, is not a fix to get rid of it altogether but a 40 percent reduction in discomfort is not to be sniffed at.

But it is not just emotions that may be blocking your path to achieving optimum self-esteem, you may also need to identify and learn to change any limiting self-beliefs that are currently stopping the "good stuff" and the things you want in your life from heading your way.

MASTERING YOUR ERRONEOUS BELIEFS

We can learn to master (and change) our belief systems that may be blocking us from restoring an optimum level of self-esteem but again, we need to know what these are and how they are stopping us from reaching our full potential.

According to British therapist, Marisa Peer, who is the founder of a technique called Rapid Transformational Therapy (and who has now trained some 4000 therapists across the globe to work with this technique) there are only ever three incorrect beliefs that can stop us from being who we really are and all three will not only damage your self-esteem but trigger some difficult emotions that can block the way to you having everything you want in your life.

These three incorrect beliefs are:

1. You are not enough
2. The "good stuff" is not available to you
3. You are different and that's why you can't connect with anyone

Can you see just how damaging these three incorrect beliefs will be when you need to build an optimum level of self-esteem and can you predict what kinds of emotions these beliefs could trigger if you allow them to persist? Believing you are not enough can only leave you feeling sad and depressed. Convincing yourself that the good stuff—which means things like happiness, love, success, and wealth—are not available to you will likely make you feel angry and resentful because that is just not fair and believing you cannot connect can feel life-threatening because connecting (to others) and avoiding rejection is how human beings have learned to stay alive and thrive. So, if this belief persists and leaves you feeling socially isolated, you will likely have to contend with some very strong feelings around that isolation, including depression and even a desire to self-harm.

A belief, however powerful or persistent, is not a fact and you already know that no amount of "believing" can make something that is false become something that is true. What is true, warns Marisa, is that if you keep on believing something, you will, eventually, make it true and prove you were right all along. But who is going to benefit from that? Certainly not you.

Those therapists trained in Marisa's technique have been taught to understand that every single problem a client brings to their door—from low self-esteem and its repercussions to addictions, and eating disorders—all stem back to one or more of these three incorrect self-beliefs, and so that is the material they work with and on in order to help someone stop self-sabotaging.

We have already seen in Part I of the book that negative self-talk can lead to a powerful but wrong negative self-image, and we explored too how we can retrain the brain to banish these beliefs and replace them with new, more positive ones.

But what can we do when we are in the midst of an emotional storm and don't have the clarity of mind or the calm, clear thinking we need to retrain the brain? The answer lies in something the ancient traditions like yoga teach us: we use the breath!

At the end of this chapter, I will show you a simple technique using the breath that will show you how to regulate your emotions this way but first, I want to look at other ways we manage our feelings, including those that can leave us feeling even worse.

OTHER SIMPLE WAYS TO MANAGE DIFFICULT EMOTIONS

We know now that allowing yourself to feel difficult emotions and, by doing this, accepting them, is a big part of preventing them from overwhelming you. But, there are other ways to stop strong emotions from derailing us. Here are some you can try next time there's a maelstrom heading your way;

1. Take stock—think about what, if any, aspects of this situation you can change, and accept the ones you can't. You always have more of a say than you think.

2. Reach out and ask for help—remember when we talked about Inspirational Relationships way back at the start of the book? This may be a friend, a trusted work colleague, or a family member. Remember too how asking for help is a strength, not a weakness and so don't delay. Reach out and ask for the help you need.

3. Don't make mountains out of molehills—some people say "don't sweat the small stuff" and mean the same thing. Try to avoid hurtling straight into panic mode when really, nothing terrible has happened and nobody's world is about to end.

4. Keep a written record of your emotions and the feelings that go with them—over time, you may be able to spot some behavioral patterns that you may wish to change or work on.

5. Listen to your body—your mind has a way to get your attention and that is to use your physical body. If you feel overwhelmed by sadness how do you know that? Because you get a lump in your throat! Pay attention to these signals and to where, in the body, different emotions like to make themselves known

6. Take regular exercise—there is no better stress-buster and no quicker way of stopping an emotional tidal-wave in its tracks than by doing something physical and distracting. Go for a walk, go for a swim. Go and volunteer in a community garden. Get off the couch and move your physical body which will help calm your mind and diffuse strong emotions.

HARMFUL WAYS TO TRY TO CONTROL DIFFICULT FEELINGS

We have all developed strategies to try to cope with difficult emotions, but some of these strategies were formed in childhood when we were not capable of the kind of adult-thinking needed to ensure our strategies are helpful and not harmful. Unfortunately, that can mean you have already adopted one or more of the following to help you cope with powerful feelings like sadness and anger and which all focus on one thing: numbing the feelings.

DENIAL

This always seems like a good idea at the time because if we pretend something is not happening and we are not struggling with difficult emotions about it. Hopefully, in time, the thing that is upsetting is and the feelings that go with it will just go away. They will disappear —but not because you have processed them and let go. They simply go "underground" and wait for the next time you feel the same way and release them. The trouble with this strategy is it means each time you let a particular feeling out, it comes out stronger than the time before. The only way to diffuse this feeling is to accept it, feel it, accept yourself and know that it will, in time, pass. Because all things, in time, will pass.

WITHDRAWAL

There are so many reasons as to why someone may start withdrawing from social interaction, and unfortunately, none of them are healthy. Withdrawal is not the same as choosing to spend some "alone" or "me" time but is more a rejection of others to protect the self, and can also be seen as a precursor to serious depression. People withdraw because they think others don't like them (low self-esteem) or because they have behaviors they feel ashamed of (hiding Real You). They may withdraw because they feel overwhelmed by their own feelings about themselves and their circumstances, or because they feel they have failed in some way. Withdrawal always causes more problems than it solves because it leads to depression, isolation, loneliness, and distorted thinking. Human beings need the input of other human beings to stay balanced.

SUBSTANCE USE

This simply means using alcohol or other drugs to numb the pain of difficult emotions and feelings to blot them out or, if you prefer, push them back down into your subconscious where you don't have to feel them. This is always a harmful and short-term solution and not least because it can lead to addiction because with these substances, it takes more and more, over time, to get to the same level of blotting out or numbing of the pain. It can also make the situation worse by intensifying difficult feelings, leading to thoughts of self-harm and even suicide.

BULLYING

Bullying is always about feeling powerless and trying to compensate for those feelings of inadequacy by imposing your will on someone else. So, bullying is always about power. It is also about making someone else feel badly about themselves so that you can feel better about yourself. Therefore, it is harmful to all involved. It is never a solution to feeling unable to cope with difficult emotions and/or low self-esteem and self-worth.

SELF-HARMING

People who self-harm do so because they feel it gives them some control over emotional pain. Cutting is the thing everyone thinks of first when we talk about self-harming, but there are multiple ways to engage in these risky behaviors which can threaten your well-being; you may starve yourself, binge, or purge. If you are using any form of self-harm to overpower painful feelings, then you already know what works for you and probably want to stop, but don't know how. If this is the case, then please reach out to someone you trust and get them to help you to get help.

NAMING DIFFICULT FEELINGS WHICH CAN FEEL SHAMING

If I asked you to make a list of the emotions (and feelings) that feel so strong they could derail you, which emotions would be on that list? You'd probably say angry or sad or stressed or anxious. You might even admit to depression too but there will be other secondary feelings, most of which are a result of not managing the primary ones in a healthier way that can also send us spiralling into losing our perspective and hating ourselves.

And these are the feelings NOBODY likes talking about, let alone admitting to.

You will probably have your own list and if you do, write that list down somewhere now. If not, you can share mine and just expand on the list below if I have not included some emotion or resultant feeling you are currently struggling to master.

FEELING LONELY, SAD, AND EMPTY

Social pain is every bit as real as physical pain, and that means it hurts the same. Neuroscientist Matthew Liberman is the author of a book called *Social* in which he explores our deeply rooted need for connection and concludes that it is as fundamental for our survival as our need for food and water. Scientists now know that we use a different part of our brain for social thinking—trying to work out what's going on inside someone else's head—than we do for analytical thinking.

If we think about the language of social pain, the clues are all there. We say things like, "She broke my heart" and, "He hurt my feelings." We acknowledge, in our language, that emotional pain is real. So why would we need an entirely different part of the brain, a distinct neural network, to help us "mind read" others and adapt our behavior accordingly?

This can only be an evolutionary function and can only mean that maintaining social ties is crucial, not only for our happiness but for our very survival. This allows us to cooperate and collaborate with others. In turn, it shapes our own behaviors and choices.

Social harmony is achieved when we surround ourselves with people who share our beliefs and values. Maintaining social harmony is a way of preventing the utter devastation we feel when our most important social ties are severed or even just threatened.

Loneliness, for example, has nothing to do with being alone. It is a state of mind which can be crippling for those who suffer from it. But even then, loneliness does not mean the same thing to everyone who suffers it. A child who is struggling to make friends at school is not feeling the same loneliness as a senior whose spouse of 50 years has just died.

Loneliness has multiple possible causes, including depression, which can lead to withdrawal, which can lead to loneliness and low self-esteem where we stay away from social connections because we believe we are not worthy of anyone else's time and attention. If allowed to go on for a long time, loneliness and the feelings of isolation and emptiness that accompany it can have a serious adverse effect on your health including:

- Increased risk of alcoholism and drug use
- Altered brain function and wrong thinking
- Acceleration of Alzheimer's disease if you are a sufferer
- Trigger for antisocial behaviors
- Increased risk of cardiovascular disease and stroke
- Lower ability to learn and remember things
- Higher risks of depression and suicide
- Increased stress levels
- Poor decision-making

Social harmony and healthy social connections can help banish loneliness and the feelings of sadness and emptiness that follow in its wake so one effective antidote to loneliness is to make a stronger connection with our Inspirational Relationships and with those who can persuade us we have an integral value and as much right to happiness and the "good stuff" as anyone else.

FINDING NO MEANING IN LIFE ANYMORE

Feelings of emptiness are another emotional challenge which can threaten to overwhelm us, especially when these feelings persist beyond the event that triggered them. If you lose someone you love and are in the middle of a bereavement, you may be feeling empty inside, but eventually, your grief will allow you to reconnect with life. When chronic feelings of emptiness persist they strip away any sense that life has meaning and that makes it hard to get up and go on each and every day.

Finding meaning in your life is crucial for your self-esteem and well-being.

Viennese psychiatrist Viktor Frankl was a Nazi concentration camp survivor who recognized, during his time in the labor camps, the human need to find meaning in life, even during the worst kind of hardships. He went on to develop logotherapy which is named after the Greek word "*logos*" meaning finding and having "meaning" in your life.

His three core beliefs are as follows:

1. Each person has a healthy core
2. The primary focus is to enlighten a person to their own internal resources and provide them with the tools to use their inner core
3. Life offers you purpose and meaning; it does not owe you a sense of fulfillment or happiness

And one of the core logotherapy treatment techniques is to redirect your attention away from yourself to look outside your internal world and become whole again by finding meaning in the world around you and thinking about something other than you and your problems. And another core idea is that your happiness, ultimately, is your responsibility.

Feeling empty can be a sign of serious mental health issues including depression, or addiction, or having borderline personality disorder. Feeling empty when you are in a relationship can be a sign it is time to cut your losses and move on.

The real message here is that feeling empty is not a feeling you should just ignore. If this feeling persists, seek help because it won't go away on its own, and it will cause damage to your self-esteem if you let it dominate your feelings and thoughts.

SOCIAL ISOLATION AND DEPRESSION

Social isolation can trigger loneliness and feelings of emptiness but there are many, many other causes of depression, and one of those is a low sense of self-worth and self-esteem. Here are some others that may resonate with you;

- Family history of depression
- Early childhood trauma or abuse
- Alcohol or drug abuse

- Marital or relationship problems: balancing the pressures of career and home life
- Family responsibilities such as caring for children, spouse, or aging parents
- Experiencing discrimination at work or not reaching important goals
- Losing your job
- Retirement
- Persistent money problems
- Death of a loved one
- Any other life event that makes you feel useless, helpless, alone, or profoundly sad.

One of the challenges of dealing with depression is that it requires energy and some sense of self-worth to set about tackling the problem, but when you are in the grip of depression, you don't have either that energy or those feelings of self-worth. You have no energy and no self-esteem.

So what can you do?

HEALTHIER WAYS OF DEALING WITH DEPRESSION

- Reach out to your Inspirational Relationships and ask for support
- Take care of your physical health: try to sleep and eat well
- Take some exercise, even a gentle walk will change your mood
- Challenge your negative self-talk and Inner Critic (go back to the start of this book and remind yourself of all the ways you can successfully do this)
- Try and get some fresh air and sunlight and avoid being cooped up all day indoors; your depression can become worse during winter when daylight hours reduce and we get less sunlight on our bodies. This is called Seasonal Affective Disorder (SAD) or you may just think of it as the Winter Blues. It is especially a risk for women who suffer from SAD four times more than men
- Check your iron levels. Low iron can cause low energy and a flagging mood spiral
- If your depression is triggering thoughts of suicide or other self-harm get professional help. Sometimes we need another person's brain and insight to help guide us out of the spiral of depression and low self-esteem

STRESS & ANXIETY

We have seen in the chapter where we looked at retraining the brain to store more positive thoughts and experiences that our thinking impacts our behaviors and our behaviors impact our thinking.

For example, just by thinking about good things in your life you can turn negative and anxious feelings into positive arousal. Say you have agreed to go to the gym with a friend. When the time comes to meet at the gym, you don't want to go, but you don't want to let your friend down. So, you turn up and remember how great you feel when you've done a challenging workout. Making ourselves do things we don't initially want to do can lead to a change in thinking and demonstrates that we can control both our thinking and our behaviors.

Now think about someone who loses their job. This is a major stress trigger and can also seriously dent someone's self-confidence and self-esteem. Our jobless friend has two choices about how they think about the position they now find themselves in: one choice will generate more fear and negativity and make the mountain ahead higher and harder to climb. The other choice will generate feelings of optimism and positivity, and it will feel easier to find their way back into employment even though the challenge is exactly the same.

We know now that our thoughts, emotions, and behaviors will follow the path we want them to follow so here is a fantastic tip for reducing stress and anxiety, whatever has triggered these powerful feelings.

Make the choice to see things in your life as challenges and your thoughts and feelings will take you in a positive and constructive direction.

When you choose to see the challenges that come your way as threats to your health, happiness, or livelihood, your thoughts and feelings will follow in a negative and destructive direction.

It really is as simple as that. You have a choice to make and what you choose will either help you master difficult emotions or leave you flailing around at their mercy.

You choose.

GETTING STUCK IN SELF-PITY

Again, we have a choice.

Did you know that scientists now claim that getting stuck in a feeling of self-pity is as bad for your health as smoking 20 cigarettes a day? It is natural to feel upset and wounded when things go wrong and perfectly acceptable to feel sorry for yourself for a few days while you lick your wounds, but beware the trap of getting stuck in the abyss of self-sorrow.

Keeping your focus on self-pity is a surefire way of triggering even more stress and anxiety. Yes, it can feel good—reassuring even—playing the victim for a few days. You might notice who is around to take extra care of you. But even the most patient of those who care about you will get tired if you don't begin to place your focus elsewhere.

Why Me? is the war cry of those stuck in self-pity. *Why did this happen to me? Why does this always happen to me?*

There is a short answer to these questions which is *Why not you?*

But by the time you've spent a week or so stuck in self-pity you will have found the answers and told yourself this happened because you're just not good enough. And there you are, back to one of Marisa Peer's top three erroneous beliefs about yourself.

Here are some techniques you can use to let go of self-pity and get yourself unstuck from victim mode:

- Allow yourself to feel compassion for yourself. Something bad has happened which has upset/derailed you and you do need time to lick your wounds—but limit that timeframe.
- Feeling hurt and sad is a normal response to things you find hurtful. Sliding into self-pity won't help you manage those difficult feelings any better. It might feel good blaming everyone and everything else for a while but eventually you will have to face the fact life can sometimes be tough.
- Refuse to be a victim. It can be quite enjoyable feeling more important for a while because there are people who feel

sorry for you, but this is not a strategy for long term happiness or success. Eventually, the people who care about you will tire of the victim persona you have adopted and even start to feel manipulated by you into showing how much they care. Nip this behavior in the bud right now before it becomes addictive, which it will.

- Understand that your perception shapes your reality. If your perception is that you deserve the bad things that happen to you, then your self-esteem will suffer. If your perception is that everyone has challenges to face in life and this event happens to be one of yours, then you will stop blaming yourself and your self-esteem can stay strong.

- Change your "*Why*" questions into *"How"*, *"What"*, and *"When"* questions. So, instead of asking yourself *Why me?* ask, *How has this happened to me and what can I do to stop it from happening again?*

FREE YOURSELF FROM GUILT & SHAME

This is another place where it is all too easy to get stuck and forget all the good work we have been doing to build an optimum level of self-esteem. If we are not careful, we can find ourselves trapped by uncomfortable feelings of guilt and shame.

Shame is universal and universally uncomfortable, and yet we somehow believe if we can just shame ourselves into doing/behaving/thinking better, we will become a better person and a person more worthy of love and respect. We will have more self-esteem.

The problem with this idea is that it is not only wrong, it is a biological impossibility to shame yourself (your brain) into changing for the better. This is because those parts of the brain that are activated by feelings of shame shut down those parts of the brain that light up ready to learn and facilitate change.

You cannot change if you are going to stay stuck with shame.

So, how do we get around this conundrum? We practice something called mindfulness which keeps the brain's learning centres open and paves the way for positive and lasting changes.

HOW MINDFULNESS CHANGES OUR BRAINS

Dr. Shauna Shapiro has been studying mindfulness ever since she found herself sitting with Thai monks trying (and failing) to meditate. Every time she followed the instruction to focus on the breath, she found her mind wandering off in a million different directions.

Dr. Shapiro did not know then what she knows now which is, according to research by scientists at Harvard University, we all have minds that wander and not only that, they wander 47 percent of our waking time. Which means we are not really present in the moment for half of our waking lives!

Happily for Dr. Shapiro, a new monk arrived from London who spoke English and told her something she says she never forgot; he said *"What you practice grows stronger."*

He then pointed out she wasn't practising mindfulness at all, she had been practising judgement, self-criticism, and impatience because she had been beating herself up mentally for failing to meditate properly.

Today, Dr. Shapiro shares her knowledge on mindfulness with audiences around the world and explains that once she understood whatever she practised would "grow" she decided to make that practice one of loving kindness, instead of harsh self-criticism and unkind thoughts.

Those Thai monks knew, from experience, what neuroscientists have discovered: the thoughts and actions we practice the most create new neural networks in the brain, and those networks then fire off positive or negative thoughts, along with mood boosting or mood dampening brain chemicals.

When we feel shame, for example, the brain sends out a cascade of the stress chemical norepinephrine, but when we feel kindness, it delivers the feel-good brain chemical dopamine to lift our mood.

So again, we can choose. What do we want to feel? Stress and anxiety triggered by shame and norepinephrine—or loving kindness and compassion, toward ourselves and toward others which will trigger a flush of feel-good dopamine?

In the simple mindfulness exercise below, you can experience this for yourself.

MINDFUL BREATHING IN (AND OUT) OF STRONG EMOTIONS

Next time you feel you are about to be overwhelmed by difficult and painful emotions, take time out to try this simple breathing exercise which will help you to accept, regulate and diffuse those feelings and remind you that you—nothing and nobody else—is the person in charge of your life and how you feel.

Find somewhere quiet to sit, somewhere you will not be disturbed for 20 minutes.

Close your eyes and bring your attention to your breathing.

Breath in through the nose and breath out through the mouth.

Purse your lips which will help slow down the breath as you exhale.

Now, as you breathe in, see if you can identify in your body where these strong emotions are signalling for your attention.

If you are sad, you may be feeling a tightness in your chest or a lump in your throat.

If you are angry, you may have a thumping headache.

If you are nervous, your stomach may be turning cartwheels somersaults.

In your mind, keep your attention on this part of your body and just feel what it is saying and what emotion it is trying to alert you to.

If you feel your mind wandering, bring it back to your breath. Count slowly as you inhale, 1. 2. 3. 4.

And count slowly as you exhale; 1. 2. 3. 4. 5. 6.

Keep your eyes closed and keep practising this mindful breathing exercise until you can feel you are calmer, your breath is calmer, your mind is calmer and the part of the body you have been giving your attention to has become less tense and more relaxed.

You can practice this exercise whenever strong emotions threaten to overwhelm you.

IN THE NEXT CHAPTER

- In the next step, **Step 10**, you will learn how to dump all the old insecurities that may be stopping you from building optimum levels of self-esteem.

STEP 10

DUMP YOUR OLD INSECURITIES

L et's see how we are doing with our self-esteem before we dive deeper into the reasons we may still be struggling.

The most popular measure still used by psychologists all over the world to measure self-esteem is the Rosenberg Self-Esteem Scale, which you can now use to assess yourself.

Work your way through these 10 questions and mark your answers as:

Strongly agree (1) Agree (2)
Disagree (3) Strongly disagree (4)

Try and answer each of the eight questions as honestly as you can.

1. I feel I am a person of worth, at least on an equal basis with others
2. I feel I have a number of good qualities
3. All in all, I am inclined to feel I am a failure*
4. I am able to do things at least as well as most other people
5. I feel I do not have much to be proud of*
6. I take a positive attitude toward myself

7. On the whole, I am satisfied with myself
8. I wish I could have more respect for myself*
9. I certainly feel useless at times*
10. At times, I think I am no good at all*

*These are reverse-scored questions which means you score higher the more strongly you disagree with the statement.

If you are still not scoring as highly as you would hope on the self-esteem scale, then it is likely your deep-seated insecurities are still getting in the way, so now is the time to dump those. Don't waste any time bearing yourself up for having them in the first place—we all have insecurities and doubts—it's just that some people have more than others, and if you want to work out where you fit on that spectrum, then you need to take a honest look at your behaviors, especially those that tell other people you are insecure.

For example, are you a people pleaser to the extent of ignoring your own needs? Are you defensive when people challenge you? Nobody likes criticism, but a secure person can face the fact they (like everyone else) is flawed and can tolerate constructive criticism because they know they can learn from it.

The telltale signs of being insecure in women are signs that can lead to endangering their lives, so we have to take this seriously. An insecure woman, for example, will stay in an abusive relationship, whereas a secure woman will have the self-confidence and self-esteem she needs to find the courage to leave.

There are two other key ways that an insecure woman may inadvertently give away that she is not as confident as she pretends; one is using humor and the other is using her body.

Humor can be helpful in diffusing difficult situations and powerful emotions, but when humor is being used to deflect from dealing with emotional issues and when someone jokes around at someone else's expense, then you can bet your bottom dollar insecurity is to blame.

The same applies when you notice a woman is overtly sexual and is using her body to get attention from men. We know sexual attraction is a powerful driver—that's why advertisers use sex to sell everything from perfume to fast cars. A secure woman does not need constant validation or to be told how beautiful and sexy she is. Her self-esteem comes from her own self-respect, and while she will enjoy a compliment, she does not need one to validate her own worth.

Unfortunately, all insecurities, even those that may have been dormant for years, become amplified in relationships. Studies suggest people attract a partner who ranks at about the same level when it comes to insecurity, so that means the insecure get together and the more secure date each other.

In this chapter, I'll show you how to ditch the worst of your insecurities. Then, if you are in the dating game, watch and see how you begin to attract healthier relationships because both partners—you and the other person—feel secure with each other and in yourselves.

Feeling secure with each other is important because studies also show the two things that most women feel insecure about are:

1. Their appearance
2. Their primary romantic relationship

Sadly, insecurities around money, career, and even creativity rank way lower than these two concerns.

WHAT WOMEN ADMIT TO FEELING INSECURE ABOUT

Sexuality: Women want is, most of all, to be thought of as sexually desirable, and they spend a lot of time measuring their perceived sexual attractiveness against that of other women.

Age: Women are insecure about their age and, if resources allow, spend a lot of time and money trying to look younger and buying into "anti-aging" products.

Weight: Women always want to be skinnier and have been programmed to believe "The thinnest woman in the room always wins!"

Breasts: Women with lower cup sizes who are bombarded by images of large-breasted celebrities want bigger breasts.

Take another look at the list above. Which of these things can you change? Yes, you can, if you can afford it, have breast augmentation surgery, but would you be going under the knife for you and your well-being or to attract a mate because you think breast size matters to men? The truth is that it does to some and not to others.

How about your age? Ask yourself this, what is the alternative to getting older? The answer is not getting older in other words, losing your life. We age or we die. Simple.

And finally what about your weight? While you can definitely take steps to get in shape and stay trimmed and toned, but skinny for skinny's sake is never a worthwhile goal. Your physique may not suit being a size 0. Even if you starve yourself to reach that goal, you will be causing untold damage to your underlying health, even risking an eating disorder like anorexia.

EMOTIONAL INSECURITIES

Other triggers that can leave us feeling insecure include a recent failure or rejection, finding ourselves in a social situation where we feel out of our depth, or setting ourselves such unrealistically high standards of unachievable perfection we are bound to fail, thus losing confidence and starting feeling insecure again.

If you are still not sure whether insecurities are blocking your path to building and maintaining an optimum level of self-esteem, here are three more telltale signs that it might be time for you to now dump the insecurities.

1. You get jealous easily
2. You become controlling when you are scared that you may not be enough
3. You take people-pleasing to a whole new level

HOW TO GET RID OF YOUR INSECURITIES FOR GOOD

Firstly, you need to recognize your insecurities haven't just landed from outer space—there will be good reasons for you feeling the way you do and for why something like rejection or getting into a new relationship triggers the old insecurities all over again.

But whatever those reasons are, don't waste your time playing the blame game because you cannot change what has gone; the future hasn't happened yet, and so the only thing you can control is yourself in the here and now.

Go back to the previous chapter and read again what the globally successful therapist Marisa Peer says about erroneous beliefs that hold us back—and what is the worst of these? It is the belief that you are not enough.

Somebody somewhere has sown this seed of an idea into your (probably) young mind, and ever since, what may have been a careless comment or some form of toxic hyper-parenting, you have developed the idea you are not and never will be enough.

If you can be honest enough to sit down with Real You, then see if you can work out where and when this belief started. Get curious about your insecurities. Put on your detective badge and follow the leads to track down what really happened to make you feel this way.

And then, just like a detective, you can begin to figure out whether your insecurities are based in truth and fact, or whether they are red herrings placed in your mind by external events to simply throw you off the scent of what really matters and who you really are.

You will also then be able to answer this all-important question: are you insecurities based in reality or are they mostly based in fear?

Once you have a better understanding of your insecurities, where they have come from and which ones have no basis in experience or reality, you can weed out those that have no real substance and no purpose other than preventing you from living your best life. You can then use the following steps to tackle those insecurities that are more persistent but which can still be eliminated once you know how.

Talk about your insecurities: If you are in a primary relationship which is being affected by your insecure behaviors, find the courage to talk honestly with your partner about what is going on and why. For example, if you identified that you feel scared your partner will suddenly abandon you, and you worked out that you legitimately feel that way because this happened with your ex, then tell your partner this is the case, and that this insecurity is a real one. If you are not in a relationship, but you have worked out insecurities are stopping you from enjoying an optimum level of self-esteem, talk to one of your Inspirational Relationship people. See if you can figure out together how to change your mindset and stop believing you are not enough.

Focus on the good stuff: One sure-fire way of sending your insecurities packing is to throw the "good book" at them, by which I mean fire one shot after another of every wonderful attribute you have, everything you have every achieved, every kind word someone has spoken about you and every kind deed you have done for someone else. "Big Up" those wins—past and present—and don't be shy about naming them. In fact, make a list when you have finished doing this of 10 things you like about yourself, and don't sell yourself short by stopping at just 5 or 6 things. Write down 10.

Take steps to find and do more of the good stuff: You're starting to see now what works in your life to help you build self-worth and self-esteem and that the more you do of that the easier it is to manage feelings of self-doubt and insecurity. What makes you feel good about yourself? Whatever it is, do more of it, and see how that quickly helps to keep self-doubt in check.

Stop comparing yourself to others: Take a digital detox and keep off the social media platforms that encourage us all to pretend our lives are just that little bit brighter and shinier than they really are. Stop comparing yourself upwards—which we have seen means thinking everyone else is having a better life than you because they are prettier, thinner, richer, younger, or more confident. Focus instead on what is good about your life and your achievements to date.

Dumping your insecurities will take time, so don't expect overnight miracles, but do stay on the case. When those insecurities crop up— and you now know the telltale signs from the first part of this chapter, you can quietly put them out of their misery and out of your life for good!

IN THE NEXT SECTION

- In Part III we take our last three steps toward building optimum self-esteem and learn how to take control, heal and understand our true value.

PART III

ENJOYING YOUR OPTIMUM LEVEL OF SELF-ESTEEM

STEP 11

HEAL. LET GO. MOVE FORWARD

"Renew, release, let go. Yesterday's gone. There's nothing you can do to bring it back. You can't "should've" done something. You can only DO something. Renew yourself. Release that attachment. Today is a new day!"

— STEVE MARABOLI, LIFE-CHANGING
SPEAKER

We touched very briefly on the idea of holding on to pain and victimhood in Step 9, and how whilst it might be gratifying to be the centre of attention for a while and see how much people love and care about us, eventually the victim tale wears thin and everyone gets bored of it. This is by no means meant to undermine the seriousness of painful events that have happened to you in your life, but we also saw in Part 1 how the brain loves to store and archive the bad stuff but how we can take deliberate steps to change that.

This Step 11 is all about healing, and in order to heal, we have to let go.

Once we let go of past hurts, we are free to move forward, keep building our optimum level of self-esteem, and then enjoy all the wonderful benefits that come with a stable and secure sense of self-worth, self-esteem, and self-directed purpose.

You have worked hard through all the previous steps of our 13-Step Program to build an optimum level of self-esteem and the final three steps that make up Part III are about rewarding your efforts and steps you've taken so far.

Part III of the book is the "feel good" section because if anyone deserves to feel good now, it is you.

And everything that I will share with you in this important Step 11 is designed to help you take one gigantic step—a step toward sustainable self-healing.

LETTING GO OF PAST HURTS

It takes an enormous amount of energy to hold on to past hurts and to hold grudges against those who have hurt us, so imagine if, instead of nursing those wounds for the rest of our lives, we were to divert that energy into something more positive and life-enhancing. And ask yourself this: by holding on to this pain, how am I helping myself to live a full and happy life?

The short answer to that question is that you're not. In fact you are doing the opposite.

Do you remember Viktor Frankl who we talked about in Step 9? He is the Nazi concentration camp survivor who went on to establish logotherapy, a school of therapy that focuses on finding meaning in our lives in places outside ourselves and our stories.

Having survived the hardships of the concentration camps, Viktor learned an important and profound lesson that underpinned all the work he did thereafter, and he was often quoted sharing this invaluable and hard-won insight. What Viktor learned was this;

> "Everything can be taken from a man but one thing: the last human freedoms—to choose one's attitude in any given set of circumstances, to choose one's own way."

— VIKTOR FRANKL

Once you understand this profound insight, you understand that your healing is in your own hands, and all you have to do is to actively choose it. Each and every day.

You can practice this by adopting a positive mantra in your life by deciding to choose peace and happiness and self-worth.

You can even say this—say these words—over and over to yourself when those buried reminders of your past "hurts" surface once more (which they will do) and threaten to upset your mood and your day.

This is not the same as pretending these things have not happened to you. They have and they are part of your story now. But as motivational speaker Steve Maraboli says in quote at the start of this chapter, yesterday is gone. You cannot go back and rewrite your story either to eliminate all the hurts or to change how you responded but you can think back and see how you have survived and become a bigger person along the way; bigger because you now have more life experience and bigger because you (hopefully) choose not to hurt back when other people wronged you.

Just imagine, it really is as easy as that. You can choose to let go and move on in just the same way you can open your fridge, see a delicious food item that is well past its sell-by date, and without a second thought, throw it out.

You wouldn't dream of eating rotting food, and there is no need to chow down any more on old wounds, and insults, and abandonments, and rejections, and heartbreaks, and other painful events.

What's more, as Steve reminds us, the only person who can let these old hurts go is you, and the very best time to release those attachments is right now, in the present moment and in the one thing you can count on: today.

It takes commitment to let go and move on but here's the good news, you have been clinging on to the past and your old stories for so long you have more than demonstrated your capacity for long-term commitment. You now just need to change what you are committing too and change it to committing to a new story: one where you have integrated old wounds and can now use them as a learning opportunity to grow.

We've seen, in Step 9 where we learned to master our more difficult emotions that resistance is futile, and ironically, the first step in letting go is always going to be acknowledging, then accepting those feelings of pain.

So here is the magic formula for releasing pain in order to move on.

Acknowledge—Accept—Forgive—Release—Move On—Grow

MOVING ON PEACEFULLY FROM YOUR PAST

When we decide to move on and leave not only our victim mentality but all the blame and shame feelings in the past where they belong, we will wake one morning and realize we feel lighter. It is as if we have left a burden on the roadside and no longer have to carry it with us wherever we go.

Here are some of the peaceful and loving ways you can learn to move on, with hope in your heart, from the bad stuff whether that is a relationship now ended, a job that has been lost, a dream not yet fulfilled, or any other disappointment, be it a failure or rejection.

Release regrets: It is important you can express and voice your feelings of regret, but don't get stuck inside them. It is important you learn to live with regrets but also to see that failure can be your most important teacher. Instead of wallowing in the pain of regret, ask yourself what you learned from this disappointment and what you would like to do differently next time.

Forgive yourself: Do not waste time travelling down the road of "If Only", meaning "If only I had never done this/met them/started that job/moved cities/confided in that friend." The only thing waiting for you at the end of his long road is yet more pain and regret. You are human, and humans (including you) make mistakes and can be forgiven. Forgiving yourself is the first step toward loving yourself, and loving yourself is the single big step you must take in order to find a healthy and sustainable new love in your future.

Recognize nothing is ever a waste of your time: Focus on the positives. However much time has passed, you have not wasted it. You have learned and you have grown. Be grateful for the chance to do what Viktor Frankl did, and choose how you see the path you have trodden to get you to where you are now. Ask anyone who has the benefit of five or six decades of life already, and they will tell you it is extraordinary how things that may have felt like harsh and pointless lessons in your life turn out to have prepared you for another chapter further down the road of your ongoing life story.

Remember the good, as well as the bad: It can sometimes feel too painful to acknowledge what was good about what we have lost, and so it is easier to just keep playing the tape of everything that was bad. But this is all-or-nothing thinking, and we saw right at the start of this book that this is just another version of wrong thinking. It may be you are among the 20 percent of the population that suffer from what researchers now call "complicated grief" which is where we can't let go because we have romanticized what's gone before and forgotten there was anything wrong with the relationship/job/person. Keep a balanced perspective and let the good go, along with the bad.

Let yourself feel everything: Grief is a well-trodden path and the various stages have been well documented: shock/denial/anger/bargaining/acceptance. The trouble is, we don't pass through these stages either in a linear fashion or just once and we don't all grieve at the same time or at the same pace. Trust the process because it is a process, and trust you will come out the other side because you will.

Remember the benefits of moving on: Holding onto pain is just another way of prolonging your suffering. Don't you think you have suffered enough? It is tortuous to obsess and rehash every painful detail, it is overwhelming to get stuck in regret and shame and guilt. Don't allow that to happen. Imagine, if you will, all of these feelings passing through you and on out into the ether. You have experienced them and that has helped you to learn and grow but there is no need for you to clear out the spare room and give them the key to your home to come and go as they please.

ALLOWING NICE THINGS TO HAPPEN

When you start to let go of your painful past, something very unexpected will happen, and before you know it, you will be asking yourself how come you never let go sooner so that you could experience all the good things that can now come your way because you have done the work and can now let go.

Here are just some of the treats in store for you now.

- There is a new, more positive version of Real You who you won't want to hide any more
- You have made space for new and good things to come into your life
- You no longer feel afraid of new challenges and the tough stuff, it is as if you have grown a special muscle to help you deal with the ups and downs of life
- You have learned to love yourself, and that is now shining brightly from inside you right out to touch everyone you meet
- This special light not only lights up the room but lights up others and helps to inspire them to discover their best selves too

- You will start to feel you are getting closer to your life purpose and your true destiny and so will be feeling more fulfilled, even if you feel you are still a work in progress
- You have more compassion and empathy for others
- You seem to be able to effortlessly attract what you need to achieve your goals and realize your dreams
- You will know in your heart and soul what is good for you and what you now need
- You will have learned that YOU are all your really need to have a happy and meaningful life
- In our penultimate Step 12 you will learn how to take control of your life

15

STEP 12

TAKE CONTROL

We live in an age of instant self-gratification—we want what we want, and we want it now—and so the very idea of developing and having self-control, including the ability to wait and work for what we want in our lives, can seem dated and old-fashioned: something our grandparents may have valued but not something we have been taught to prize.

But the truth is, as we have worked through the previous 11 steps of my 13-Step Program to Optimum Self-Esteem, we have already taken those first important steps on the path to greater self-control and discernment because we can now work out, when faced with life choices, what is good for us and what may not be.

Psychologists define self-control as using reason and rational thinking to master our instincts. It is not about denying ourselves or choosing total abstinence, but it is about not allowing our desires and wants and wishes to overwhelm us.

Learning to develop self-control is about finding the right balance between what we want, what we need, and what we are prepared to do or give us to meet those needs, and so we can think of it as a balancing act.

Did you ever hear anyone say: *A little of what you fancy does you good?* Or *All things in moderation?*

Because that's really what we are talking about here.

So, how do we apply reason to learning how to master self-control?

We do it by taking time to pause and ask ourselves the right questions before deciding on the importance of a desire/want/need and before taking steps to gratify that desire/want/need.

Here are some of the questions you can try asking yourself next time there's a voice in your head telling you to have another alcoholic drink at the party, buy the dress you know you can't afford, book the holiday that will blow a month's budget in a week, or hop into bed with the stranger who told you that you have beautiful eyes but who (you noticed) looks over your shoulder to scan the room whilst you are speaking.

HOW RIGHT THINKING HELPS BUILD SELF-CONTROL

- **How much is too much?** Ask yourself what is it you want and, just as importantly, how much of that "thing" do you want? Be honest with yourself. If it is the case that as soon as you have that "thing," you will want more or something else, then this is a red flag because nothing will ever be enough, and that way lies the painful road to addiction. This can be addiction to drugs, drama, shopping, or perhaps people who are not good for our well-being and self-esteem. You will know the familiar signs.
- **What would you do to get what you want?** Again, be honest. Would you cheat? Lie? Steal? Break the law? Break up another family? Put yourself into crippling debt?
- **How much pain will it cause to not satisfy this desire?** Ask yourself why it causes any pain and whether this desire is now so out of kilter it is damaging your enjoyment of life

and/or the enjoyment of other people. If the answer is yes, this is a desire you need to master.

- **What would happen if you delayed gratification?** If the answer is "the world will still keep spinning," then you already know this is not a life-or-death outcome. You won't die if you have to wait. You will survive if you have to exercise a little self-control.

THE GOLDILOCKS FORMULA

You know that you need to exercise self-control when you have an overwhelming desire to do something pleasurable, which you know will not be good for you, especially in excess. Equally, you need to exercise self-control when the idea of doing something that is good for you fills you with disgust.

As you ask yourself the above questions, think about what, for you in your present circumstance, would be too much, too little or just right? Once you settle on "just right," you are on your way to exercising self-control.

It is human nature to want good things, to want more of them and to want them now, but once you master self-control, one of the first things you will learn is that delayed gratification has its own rewards because often, waiting for something good will deliver even more of it!

REACHING YOUR FULL POTENTIAL

Psychologists talk about an idea known as "self-actualization" which really just means setting and following your inner compass to reach your full potential and become who you really are, flaws and all.

This idea is rooted in a theory established in 1943 by the American psychologist, Abraham Maslow, who put forward his hierarchy of needs theory which reveals our motivation and shows what is important for us to survive and thrive and in what order they need to be met.

Not surprisingly, the hierarchy starts with the basics including air, food, and water. After that, says Maslow, we can pursue safety, love, belonging, and self-esteem.

"What a man can be, he must be," said Maslow. "And we can call this need self-actualization."

SETTING YOUR INNER COMPASS

If you are not sure how to set your inner compass or what this even means, it simply refers to the driving force that will, if you allow it, ensure you become precisely who you are meant to become.

If, for example, you believe you have failed because you are not the mother of 2.5 children living in a fancy house, driving an even fancier car, and holding down a demanding job, then you are not following your own compass but someone else's. None of those material-based things may be important to you, so why would you pursue them? And, even if some of them are, the fact you don't have them does not mean you have failed. Imperfection is part of being human.

Take some time to connect to your inner compass by thinking about what kind of person you do want to be and write down what is important to you.

This is your life. You are permitted to set your own compass and choose your own dreams and goals and doing this—taking agency for your life and your choices—is one of the most important steps in building a healthy and stable optimum level of self-esteem.

BECOMING SELF-ACTUALIZED

Here are some of the behaviors people with optimum self-esteem show. Copy this list somewhere where you can tick those behaviors you have now adopted as part of this 13-Step Program and circle those you are still working on. These are all the behaviors of a self-actualized person who knows who they are and what matters to them.

- Knows the difference between confidence and arrogance
- Is not afraid of feedback
- Does not people-please or seek approval

- Is not afraid of conflict
- Is able to set boundaries
- Is able to voice needs and opinions
- Is assertive, but not pushy
- Is not a slave to perfection
- Is not afraid of setbacks
- Does not fear failure
- Does not feel inferior
- Accepts who they are

IN THE NEXT CHAPTER

- In the next chapter, you will learn how to get to know your real value.

STEP 13

KNOW YOUR REAL VALUE

HAVING A SENSE OF PURPOSE

Having a sense of purpose doesn't just make you feel better about yourself and your life, research has shown it can also help you live longer. A sense of purpose is more stable and more far-reaching than the tasks on our every day "To Do" list, like putting the dinner on or taking the trash out in time for collection.

The Stanford University psychologist William Damon defined sense of purpose as:

> *"A stable and generalized intention to accomplish something that is at once meaningful to the self and of consequence to the world beyond the self."*

And so this definition tells us that a sense of purpose involves, in some way, reaching beyond yourself. It involves achievement, progress and completion and will result in supporting your self-esteem and sense of self-value and self-worth.

"Purpose" does not have specific boundaries or limitations, so whether you experience yours as a volunteer, a receptionist, a teacher, a caretaker, a parent, or a doctor does not matter. What matters is having a sense of purpose because this is the cornerstone of happiness, optimal well-being, and having a life well-lived.

In your notebook, make a list now of the things you do or have done that have made you feel this way. These will be the things that have given your life meaning. If you can find what has meaning for you, then you can use that sense of purpose to build an optimum level of self-esteem.

THE NIAGARA SYNDROME

According to the motivational speaker, Tony Robbins, too many of us suffer from something he called "The Niagara Syndrome" where we let our lives flow by like a meandering river, failing to make a plan, decide where we want the river to take us and, by default, never consciously making those important decisions.

He describes how many of us jump on the river of life without ever really deciding where we want to end up and how this means we get caught up in the current: current events, current fears, and/or current challenges.

This also means, when we come to a fork in the river, we don't decide where we want to go or which is the right direction for us. We simply go "with the flow," becoming part of the group of people who allow external circumstances, rather than their own internal values, to direct them. And when this happens, we feel out of control. What Robbins says about this is:

They remain in this unconscious state until one day, the sound of the raging water awakens them, and they discover they're five feet from Niagara Falls in a boat with no oars," warns Tony. "At this point they say, "Oh shoot!" But by then, it's too late. They're going to take a fall.

The fall can be emotional, physical or financial and if we had only consciously taken some better decisions upstream, the chances are we would have avoided any kind of fall.

What we are learning in this final step of our 13-Step Program to build your optimum self-esteem is that "purpose" is the starting point of all success, so if you want success and want to avoid those "falls," make sure you don't set out down the river until you know your purpose.

Armed with that information, you will consciously make the right decisions that will steer you in the right direction and keep you on that healthy track because your sense of purpose not only gives you meaning and motivation, it will also show you which way to go and which paths to take to realize your dreams and be able to join the group of people who can say, "I lived a good life!"

And don't ever let anyone tell you that your purpose is less important because of your gender: either assigned or the one you now identify with.

"A woman's purpose is the same as a man's purpose, to pursue an education we are so gracefully allowed and able to pursue to know themself, the universe around them and then how they can make it a better place for themselves and those around them lifting the quality of life for all, with the assistance of the all, for the all is everything."

— DEAN IRWIN

Remember, too, how we have just learned that purpose has no specific boundaries or limitations or even definitions. This means, the truth is, your purpose is whatever you want it to be.

"A woman's purpose is whatever she wants it to be unless she is restrained by the society in which she is born."

— RICHARD UTKKE

A GIRL IS BORN A MOTHER

I don't mean this, literally, of course. When I say a girl is born a mother I mean she is a refuge, a vessel, a bearer, a nurturer, a carer, an influencer, and a mediator.

You are already all those things, and so much more.

AND YOU ARE NOT JUST A WOMAN

As you set out now to find and define your true purpose—as part of building your own optimum level of a stable, healthy and sustainable self-esteem—consider this. Whilst it is true that for each of us, our sense of purpose may differ there is one purpose that we, as women, all share and that is:

To create, and not destroy.

It is important too that you start to live your passion so that you can be a shining example to others: to your sisters and friends, your work colleagues, and classmates, to the daughters you may raise and even your own mothers.

Never stop seeking growth and ways to contribute to your community and society at large.

It is your duty—and your honor—to deliver yourself, your Real Self in your true, feminized core, to all the world.

You are, and always will be, more than a woman.

OUR COMMITMENT

Let us all be advocates

Let us all be divine hands

Lift others, save others

Let us all be the heart of nature

We are all mothers

Let us all be "A woman who changed the world"

Because my darling,

You are more than just a woman

FINAL THOUGHTS

A MESSAGE TO YOU FROM SARRANA RAIN

Mother: a refuge, a vessel, a bearer, nurturer, carer, influencer, mediator,
A girl is born a mother.

To You, Dear Reader,

You can call me Sarrana.

I am a nurse (but really, this is irrelevant),

I am a woman who is on a journey of self-discovery and mastery herself.

The moment I learned to walk, I had to move from one place to another. I grew up with no parent figure; siblings were always out of reach, and so I raised my own self away from family.

I was indeed unsheltered: no roof, no walls, no light.

Since my teens, almost everything I have learned is self-taught; no warnings, no voice of guidance. And oh yes, I made huge mistakes. Most of the time, I felt like I was a wild seed that grew into a tree with no roots.

I needed a father more than a God.

Life was lonely and it has been difficult to establish "Self."

At first, it didn't bother me much; like any typical young adult, I was just busy working toward my goals everyday, and paving my way to a place from where I could live comfortably.

I successfully moved from the Philippines to the UK where, yes, life was good, yet it was only then that I started to feel the repercussions of having had no guidance.

I felt empty. I always felt empty but this time, I could feel it more.

I was rejected, I was abandoned, I couldn't belong. I lost my confidence, I lost my wit, I couldn't communicate, I couldn't understand my place.

I isolated myself and couldn't comprehend the meaning of my existence anymore.

Everyday, I wanted to just disappear. And you know what, I have been like this since the age of six, and yet I have still managed to live since then.

I lived only because I breathe.

So, I began questioning my self-worth: where is it, how much is there, did I lose it, or did I even have it in the first place?

After years of soulful quest and obsessive research, I have finally put together all the wisdom I have learned and from it, built the steps for you to climb that will also help you reach the optimum level of self-esteem—the unconditional, strong, and stable kind of self-worth. It is pretty sturdy and so should last you for a lifetime.

Life itself is very unstable, causing your ground to shake, you might fall from the steps, we all do, and when that happens, we just have to walk our way again to the top.

Together, let's make this a vision:

Women, they just have to see things in a new light, then there is the better world waiting for them, a world full of compassion wherein they can strive to hone their abilities and uniqueness, live mindfully with inner peace, make things happen with courage and will, be themselves the master of their own self- gentle but dauntless, resilient and driven, exist with a sense of purpose, cultivate love to self and others, respects self while respecting others.

I trust you to become the bigger person. Your mission after saving yourself is to give another a hand. Remember "Our Commitment": a girl is born a mother.

~

Dear woman,
I value your worth, and I deeply hope I can help you see it.
Your confidence is as important as your feet, and I sincerely hope you can unleash it.
I need you to believe in yourself. The world needs you to believe in yourself.
You need YOU to believe in yourself.

~

ACKNOWLEDGMENTS

WE NEED YOUR HELP!

We would like to deeply thank you for having this book.

It is our big hope dear reader that this book, 13 Steps to Optimum Self-Esteem for Women will reach and touch thousands of souls, changing their life for good. And we are humbly asking for your kind help to make this happen by giving this book a review on Amazon, the main place where people around the world can find it. Every review this book receives helps it climb the rankings consequently reaching more new readers within its entire existence.

We passionately read all the reviews and consider them as we update our books. We also use them to get ideas for future projects. That is how important your review will be, our dear reader.

We would be incredibly grateful if you could just take a minute, head to your Amazon account, and share your thoughts and experience, even if it's just a sentence or two. Uploading a few photographs of you and the book and/or your favourite pages will be even more convincing!

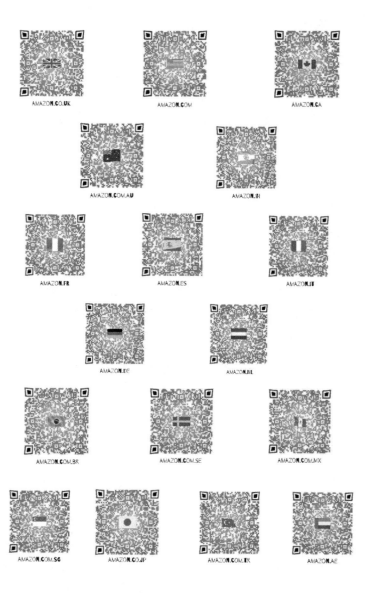

Please select the country/region website in which your account is registered, then scan the corresponding QR code with your smart phone to get into a straightforward form where you can write your precious review.

A million thanks to you for playing such a big role in the future success of this book.

And a billion thanks to these amazing characters for making this beautiful book come to life:

SUSAN CLARKE *

LUKE WRIGHT

AJAYLA JOHNSON

DIOGO LEITE

IVY MAGSIPOC

RENEE LETZ

MARTHA REINEKE

RACHEL SCHULTZ

ELIZABETH TEBB

JESSE PATTINSON

JOSE ANGULO

MAJID BAZOUYAR

FAIZAN AHMAD

ULDSON LIMA

ROCHELLE GONZALES

AIA

YOUR NEXT READ

Imagine a life in which your confidence and tranquillity come from within. Imagine waking up in love with yourself without needing validation from a man or anyone just to feel worthy, bearing an eternal belief that your worth is innate and cannot be taken away from you.

What if you no longer feel insecure about the way you look because of society's standards – that, to be feminine, we must be beautiful, educated, and maternal in a specific way.

What if you no more consider yourself 'not good enough' because you failed in the past. What if you enjoyed rather than feared new challenges and people. What if you could step outside of your comfort zone.

What if I told you there was a way to empower yourself? To lift these burdens from your shoulders and experience life without fear?

See yourself in a new light.

The meditation prompts, affirmations, and practical tips found in this book will allow you to unravel your best self. You will discover how to instil positive messaging into your mind- and that will lead to positive results in your life!

There's also a series of unique exercises for you to complete. By combining emotional and practical tasks, you are sure to enhance your self-confidence and self-esteem so that you may enjoy a fulfilled and happy life, fully accepting who you are, but open and equipped for more improvement.

This guide doesn't promote toxic positivity. It does just the opposite. It encourages you to embrace your negative emotions and teaches you how you can learn from them, move forward, and become a better person.

Despite your past, your failures, and your doubts, you have it in you to break through and reach your full potential.

If you want to reclaim your sense of self, feel empowered to achieve your goals, and be the strong, confident woman you're meant to be, then grab your own copy of the book now!

THE BOOK

BY SCANNING THE QR CODE

SCAN ME

 SARRANA RAIN

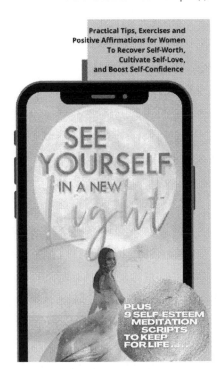

Practical Tips, Exercises and Positive Affirmations for Women To Recover Self-Worth, Cultivate Self-Love, and Boost Self-Confidence

SEE YOURSELF IN A NEW *Light*

PLUS
9 SELF-ESTEEM MEDITATION SCRIPTS TO KEEP FOR LIFE . . . .

REFERENCES

About Self-Esteem. Mind. https://www.mind.org.uk/information-support/types-of-mental-

health-problems/self-esteem/about-self-esteem/.

Abdel-Khalek, Ahmed. (2016). Introduction to the Psychology of self-esteem.

Ackerman, C. (2021). What is Self-Compassion and What is Self-Love? *Positive Psychology.*

https://positivepsychology.com/self-compassion-self-love/.

Ball, A. L. (2008). Women and the Negativity Receptor. *Oprah.com.* https://www.oprah.com/omagazine/why-women-have-low-self-esteem-how-to-feel-more-confident/all

Ball, A. L. (2019, April 9). *Women and the negativity receptor.* BrainHQ from Posit Science. Retrieved December 23, 2021, from https://www.brainhq.com/news/women-and-the-negativity-receptor/

Barber, N. (2013). Why Women Feel Bad About Their Appearance. *Psychology Today.*

https://www.psychologytoday.com/gb/blog/the-human-beast/201305/why-women-feel-bad-about-their-appearance

Berns-Zare, I. (2019) The Importance of Having a Sense of Purpose. *Psychology Today.*

https://www.psychologytoday.com/gb/blog/flourish-and-thrive/201906/the-importance-having-sense-purpose

Cherry, K. (2021). What is Self-Esteem? *VeryWellMind.* https://www.verywellmind.com/what-is-self-esteem-2795868.

Ditzfeld, C. P. & Showers, C. J. (2013) Self-Structure: the Social and Emotional Contexts of Self-Esteem. *Current Issues in Psychology: Self Esteem,* 21-42.

Dorter, G. (2020). Cognitive Fusion and Defusion in Acceptance and Commitment Therapy. *Guelph Therapist.* https://www.guelphtherapist.ca/blog/cognitive-fusion-defusion/.

Greenberg, M. (2015) The 3 Most Common Causes of Insecurity and How to Beat Them. *Psychology Today.* https://www.psychologytoday.com/gb/blog/the-mindful-self-express/201512/the-3-most-common-causes-insecurity-and-how-beat-them

Goldsmith, A. H., Veum, J. R., Darity, W. (1997). Unemployment, joblessness, Psychological Well-Being and Self-Esteem: Theory and Evidence. *The Journal of Socio-Economics,* 26(2), 133-158.

Hanson, R. (2021). The Science of Positive Brain Change. *RickHanson.net.*

https://www.rickhanson.net/the-science-of-positive-brain-change/.

Kaufman, S. B. (2018). What Does It Mean to Be Self-Actualized in the 21st Century? *Scientific American.* https://blogs.

scientificamerican.com/beautiful-minds/what-does-it-mean-to-be-self-actualized-in-the-21st-century/

Lazarus, C. (2018). How to Respond to Criticism. *Psychology Today.* https://www.psychologytoday.com/gb/blog/think-well/201802/how-respond-criticism.

Markway, B. (2019). 3 Keys to Handling Mistakes. *Psychology Today.* https://www.psychologytoday.com/gb/blog/shyness-is-nice/201904/3-keys-handling-mistakes

McKay, M, & Fanning, P. Self-Esteem - Stopping Your Inner Critic. *The Positive Way.*

https://positive-way.net/self-esteem-stopping-your-inner-critic/.

McLeod, S. (2012). Low Self Esteem. *Simply Psychology.*

https://www.simplypsychology.org/self-esteem.html.

McMullin, J. A., Cairney, J. (2004). Self-esteem and the intersection of age, class, and gender. *Journal of Aging Studies, 18(1),* 75-90.

Morgane, T. The Neuroscience of Self-Worth. *To Be Magnetic.* https://tobemagnetic.com/tbm-blog/2018/neuroscience-self-worth

Murk, C. (2006). *Self-Esteem Research, Theory, and Practice: Towards a Positive Psychology of Self Esteem* (3rd edition). Springer Publication Company.

Ngo, N. T. (2019). What Historical Ideals of Women's Shapes Teach Us About Women's SelfPerception and Body Decisions Today. *Journal of Ethics, 21 (10).* 879-901.

Nguyen, K. 7 Reasons I Was Scared to Take Up Space and How I Boosted My Confidence. *Tiny Buddha.* https://tinybuddha. com/blog/7-reasons-i-was-scared-to-take-up-space-and-how-i-boosted-my-confidence/

Self-Esteem: Take Steps to Feel Better About Yourself (2020 July 14) Mayo Clinic. https://www.mayoclinic.org/healthy-lifestyle/adult-health/in-depth/self-esteem/art-20045374

*Social Anxiety Self-Help Guide. (*2021 May 17). NHS Inform. https://www.nhsinform.scot/illnesses-and-conditions/mental-health/mental-health-self-help-guides/social-anxiety-self-help-guide

Sowislo, J. F., & Orth, U. (2013). Does low self-esteem predict depression and anxiety? A meta-analysis of longitudinal studies. *Psychological Bulletin, 139*(1), 213–240

Schwartz, A. N. The Incredible Human Brain, Neuroplasticity, and the Power of Positive Thinking. *MentalHelp.* https://www.mentalhelp.net/blogs/the-incredible-human-brain-neuroplasticity-and-the-power-of-positive-thinking/

Resilience: Build Skills to Endure Hardship. (2020 October 27). Mayo Clinic.

https://www.mayoclinic.org/tests-procedures/resilience-training/in-depth/resilience/art-20046311

Rosen, J. (2018). The Powerful Way to Overcome Fear, Doubt, and Anxiety. *Influencive.*

https://www.influencive.com/the-powerful-way-to-overcome-fear-doubt-and-anxiety/.

Vlazny, M. (2016). Understanding Women & Self-Esteem. *PsychCentral.*

https://psychcentral.com/lib/women-and-self-esteem#1.

Warrell, M. (2015). Use It Or Lose It: The Science Behind Self-Confidence. *Forbes.*

https://www.forbes.com/sites/margiewarrell/2015/02/26/build-self-confidence-5strategies/?sh=7db564006ade